T0348803

COMFORT FOR
Caregivers

COMFORT FOR
Caregivers
100 Devotions
to Lift Your Spirit

Editors of *Strength & Grace*

 Guideposts

A Gift from Guideposts

Thank you for your purchase! We want to express our gratitude for your support with a special gift just for you.

Dive into *Spirit Lifters*, a complimentary e-book that will fortify your faith, offering solace during challenging moments. Its 31 carefully selected scripture verses will soothe and uplift your soul.

Please use the QR code or go to **guideposts.org/ spiritlifters** to download.

Comfort for Caregivers: 100 Devotions to Lift Your Spirit

Published by Guideposts
100 Reserve Road, Suite E200
Danbury, CT 06810
Guideposts.org

Copyright © 2024 by Guideposts. All rights reserved.

This book, or parts thereof, may not be reproduced, stored in a retrieval system, or transmitted in any form or by any means, electronic, mechanical, photocopying, recording, or otherwise, without the written permission of the publisher.

Cover design by Beth Meyer
Cover photo by Molesko Studio, Shutterstock
Typeset by Aptara, Inc.
ISBN 978-1-961441-09-5 (softcover)
ISBN 978-1-961441-10-1 (epub)

Printed and bound in the United States of America

A Note from the Editor

"There are only four kinds of people in the world," said former US First Lady Rosalynn Carter. "Those who have been caregivers. Those who are currently caregivers. Those who will be caregivers, and those who will need a caregiver." If you're reading these pages, chances are you fall into one or more of these categories. The 100 inspiring and insightful devotions herein were taken from *Strength & Grace*, Guideposts' bimonthly devotional magazine focused on caregiving. They will help you chart your course as you tackle one of life's most difficult challenges: caring for an aging parent. The devotions brim with hope and inspiration, layered with hard-won and heartfelt advice, both practical and spiritual.

Topics we explore in this book include transitioning into a caregiving role; dealing with a parent's memory loss, dementia, or Alzheimer's; asking God for strength and hope; experiencing burnout and knowing when to ask for help; finding unexpected joy and connection in caregiving; transitioning your parent to full-time care in a nursing home or other facility; and, finally, dealing with the loss of your parent and coming to the end of a caregiving season.

As someone who was recently a caregiver for my mother, who passed away after a long bout with multiple myeloma, I now have an even greater appreciation for the challenges caregivers face, from the monitoring of medications, to the planning of meals, to the ever-important and often difficult job of keeping up morale—both yours and your loved one's.

Ultimately, God supports you in this endeavor, and He will give you strength, courage, and confidence for the journey. He lifts you up just as you are lifting those you're caring for. And the caregivers writing in these pages will lift your spirits too with their willingness to take on the tough acts of compassion. They walk you through their experiences, their successes, and even sometimes their failures. They tell you that it's OK to ask for help, to receive care just as you give it.

Guideposts writer Cookie Cranston has coined the phrase "life interrupted by life itself," and what could be more perfect to describe the season of caregiving? Interruptions, one after another—to our days, our nights, our routines, sometimes our very sanity, as the task demands. Not to mention the interruptions to our spiritual lives. But over the course of the 1,440 minutes in each day, we can find small moments of joy and slivers of insight. These "big little moments" are what you'll find in these devotions: from receiving a kind word spoken in gratitude, to enjoying a favorite television show together, to discovering a new hobby that can be enjoyed by the caregiver and their loved one. So be on the lookout for those big little moments among the 1,440 in your day today and bask in their firefly glow. After all, moments—not days or even hours—are where we live, as God intends.

Yes, it can be a tough road, but you'll see there are also many opportunities for emotional and spiritual growth, times of unsurpassed poignancy, deepening bonds with your loved ones, and, believe it or not, sometimes even a few laughs along the way. We aim to help light that path for you. Always remember that between our sunrise and our sunset, there are still so many colors in the day. You just have to look heavenward to see them.

Take care,

Kimberly Elkins
Editor, *Strength & Grace*

If you'd like to subscribe to *Strength & Grace*,
order at shop.guideposts.org/devo.

All Made in God's Image

Be devoted to one another in love. Honor one
another above yourselves. Never be lacking in zeal,
but keep your spiritual fervor, serving the Lord.
—ROMANS 12:10–11 (NIV)

Human beings, made in God's image, are all worth honoring. The word *honor* means to "treat with great respect." As a caregiver, it can be challenging at times to respect the wishes of a family member. Particularly if that person does not express gratitude or is childish and demanding. The following three principles may be helpful in difficult situations:

Remember: This person was not always the way they are today. Trauma, illness, and aging all have a way of reducing a human being to negative, possibly irritating behaviors. Choose something positive to cling to, and know you are not just serving them, you are serving the Lord.

Empower: When possible, respect and honor a person's choices, no matter how silly you might think them, as long as no one's safety is compromised. We are all unique and feel best when we have the freedom to choose.

Listen: Everyone has a story. One of the best ways to honor another person is to ask to hear their story. Be present and interested. The insight you receive into the person they are today may prove to be an unexpected blessing.

*Dear Father, help me to remember we are all made in
Your image and are thus deserving of honor. Show me
practical ways to extend respect to those in my care.*
CATHERINE MADERA

Silent Night, Sleepless Night

As a mother comforts her child, so will I comfort you.

—ISAIAH 66:13 (NIV)

Moonlight peeks through the window blinds, streaking the shadows of my darkened room. I lie in bed and listen for the sound of my mother through the baby monitor placed in her bedroom. Alzheimer's has left her unable to navigate well on her own, especially at night.

"Mom!" she yells for me.

"I'm coming," I tell her.

I'm not sure when she began calling me Mom, but our roles have reversed. Now it's me who prepares her meals just as she did for me when I was a child. Now I'm the one who soothes her back to sleep.

She is lying on the carpeted floor of her room, unhurt but scared, having fallen trying to get out of bed. She holds her arms up for me to help her. I struggle to get her back onto the mattress.

"Can I get up?" she asks.

"Let's try to sleep some more. It's the middle of the night."

"But I'm not tired."

We've gone over this same scenario night after night. I try not to cry. I haven't been this tired since my children were newborns. My exhaustion is becoming debilitating. I think back to what soothed my own children when they were restless. I begin singing "Silent Night" while rubbing her back.

Mom is asleep before I get through the second stanza. Although I'm still tired, the song has also comforted me. Singing it brought back happy memories, but I'm also making new memories that give me comfort throughout sleepless nights.

*Lord, help me to accept comfort wherever
I find it on my caregiving journey.*

JEANNIE HUGHES

A Different Lens

Do not grieve, for the joy of the L ORD is your strength.
—NEHEMIAH 8:10 (NIV)

As my father's Alzheimer's progressed, he began having trouble with tasks that required multiple steps. He would call to ask me to help him remember the order of changing his clothes. Each time, I'd slowly talk him through the steps, pausing after each step so he could put the phone down to perform it. When we'd finished, I'd hang up the phone and cry. It was painful when I'd think about this man who'd once been a college administrator having to struggle just to get dressed.

But then one day he called me back, telling me the list I had written up and posted in his bedroom had solved the problem. He was happy to say he had successfully readied himself for the day without having to make a phone call. "Thank you, babe," he said, his voice triumphant.

I realized that what might seem sad and tragic at first glance could become a positive if I looked at it through a different lens.

I had to learn that I couldn't place my expectations—or my memories of the way things used to be—on my dad. When I finally let that go, his accomplishment ended up bringing both of us joy and reminding me that no matter our situation, God always provides.

Dear God, help us to relish every victory, no matter how small.
MISSY TIPPENS

The Keys

Whether you turn to the right or to the left, your ears will hear
a voice behind you, saying, "This is the way; walk in it."
—ISAIAH 30:21 (NIV)

Sharon, I was dizzy and almost passed out driving home from the
grocery today. I don't think I should be driving."

I took a deep breath before responding. "Well, Mom, we have the
initial appointment with your cardiologist next week. If you can get
by without driving until we see the doctor, maybe we'll have more
answers then. Do you have enough groceries in to tide you over?"

Years ago, when Mom was a young mother, an elderly man ran his
car onto a sidewalk not far from where we lived. A toddler was killed.
That stuck with my mother. She had told me the story several times.
She didn't want to be that person. Ever.

This wouldn't be easy. But I was glad Mom recognized the danger
she might be to herself and others if she continued driving. For many
of my peers, taking car keys away from elderly parents caused rifts.

We worked out a plan. If Mom needed anything before I got to
visit her again, she would call one of her friends. She had a wide circle
of friends; finding someone shouldn't be a problem. But this was
only a patch. A more permanent plan was needed. "Let's pray on this,
Mom. We'll get it figured out."

*Dear Lord, be with caregivers and patients facing life-
altering decisions. Let them be open to Your voice of
love and reason when hard choices loom.*
SHARON DRACH MANGAS

Little Things Mean a Lot

He will yet fill your mouth with laughter and
your lips with shouts of joy.
—JOB 8:21 (NIV)

It's all the little things that our loved ones need that seem to be the hardest things to do sometimes. It's those things that often help the most.

I traveled to see Mom every few months, staying a few days to a week as my schedule allowed. Missy, my sister-in-law, was Mom's main caregiver. Missy welcomed a break when I could take over for a bit, especially since Mom could no longer walk.

"Would you wash my hair today?" Mom asked on my first day there.

"Certainly. Do we use the kitchen sink, or do I need to get you in the shower?"

"No, you do it right here in my recliner." I raised my eyebrows at that. "Call Missy! She knows how to do it."

"I need help already," I told Missy dejectedly on the phone. She came over and shampooed Mom's hair with a washrag and a bowl of warm water while she sat in her chair. I could do that.

A few days later, I wrapped a towel around Mom's neck and another over the back of her chair—just like Missy had done. I dipped a washrag into the water but forgot to wring it out. Water gushed over Mom's head, down her face, and onto the front of her shirt. She started laughing. I did too. We couldn't seem to stop. Ah, there she was. Mom before Parkinson's. Oh, how I missed her.

Lord, thank You for sweet moments of comfort. Let me
never forget the battle my loved one is fighting.
PAMELA HASKIN

In a Heartbeat

*I remember God, and I moan. I complain,
and my spirit grows tired.*
—PSALM 77:3 (CEB)

As a caregiver, I know what it is to grow tired and discouraged. At such times, I have found comfort in the psalmist's honest complaints, the doubting and moaning even when thinking of God. As my mother grew mentally distant with dementia, it sometimes felt like God was leaving her behind, even though I knew better. This verse helped me remember that God knows about my doubts and struggles, welcomes me to express them like the psalmist, and loves me all the same.

Sometimes, I struggled saying good night to my mother after my regular evening visits with her in the memory care unit. I wished I didn't have to leave her alone. Then I would listen to her heartbeat. For me, a heartbeat is one reassurance that God will not forsake us. Every heartbeat reassured me of God's constant, caring presence.

I cannot live without a pulse, yet I cannot keep my own heart beating. Only God can, and God does—over 100,000 times per day, 37 million times per year, even when I lie asleep. Thus, when saying good night to my mom, I would often place my ear to her heart as we hugged. Her steady pulse reassured me of God's faithful care for her, which I believe continues now in heaven.

Dear Heavenly Father, thanks for Your faithful promise never to forsake me. Help me to remember to trust that You love and care for my loved ones more than I ever could.
JEFF BJORCK

Paying Goodness Forward

Set your affection on things above, not on things on the earth.
—COLOSSIANS 3:2 (KJV)

When my father's prostate cancer spread to his bones, he had to be transported to his doctor appointments in a wheelchair. It was cumbersome to get him in and out of the car and into the doctors' offices, and it quickly wore him out.

One afternoon, I took off from work to drive Dad to a new urologist. He suggested Dad receive a monthly injection to curtail the effects of the disease. As he further examined Dad, I saw his eyes take in my father's tiredness and anguish. Suddenly, he said, "Why don't you let me stop by your house once a month to do these injections? That way, you won't have to travel all this way to see me."

Dad smiled for the first time in weeks. "You don't mean it, Doc," he said. "I didn't think you fellows made house calls anymore."

After I got Dad settled at home and returned to my job, there was a new spirit in my step. To my surprise, I heard myself offer to help a coworker with a project that far exceeded my comfort zone. As we labored over a spreadsheet, she told me, "I think I'll go home tonight and fix my husband's favorite spaghetti dinner. Who knows, he may get the energy to help our next-door neighbor with his gutters."

In matters large and small, may we pay kindness forward to those around us.

Thank You, Father, for the beautiful ripple effects of doing Your will.
ROBERTA MESSNER

Happiness in the Past or Present

"Comfort from my lips would bring you relief."
—JOB 16:5 (NIV)

All in all, my mom is still pretty with it. We only saw hints of dementia at first, but as the months have passed, we've encountered more and more challenges. Recently, she's been convinced her childhood home is a bed and breakfast. She forgets that she can't drive anymore and wants me to call the mechanic and schedule her car maintenance.

I used to remind her that she couldn't drive anymore and say that I'd driven past Grandma's home, and it definitely wasn't a bed and breakfast. I'd follow the letter of the law—not lying to her—but she'd get really upset and sometimes even scared by the truth, which conflicted with her new and changing sense of reality.

I realized it was better not to challenge her memories or what she thought was going on, as long as those beliefs weren't putting her in any danger. I've learned to say, "I don't have the phone number with me" when she asks about the mechanic and to murmur, "How nice" when she says she stayed at the bed and breakfast the night before. It doesn't matter, in the end, if she's living in the past or in the present, as long as she is happy wherever she is at the moment.

*Father, help me remember that sometimes as caregivers
we need to adjust to the new realities of our loved ones and
focus most on giving them joy and peace.*
MONICA HERALD

It Takes a Village

As those who have been chosen of God, holy
and beloved, put on a heart of compassion, kindness,
humility, gentleness, and patience.
—COLOSSIANS 3:12 (NASB)

I thank God every day for guiding my mother to the assisted memory care facility where she now resides. The people who work there are particularly wonderful and caring to her.

Yesterday when I visited Mom, her fingernails were painted. Granted, they were each painted a different color, but what a great idea to give Mom a rainbow spectrum on her hands. I knew it must be Karla's work. Then Tiffany came to me. She had noticed an issue with Mom's skin and had searched the Internet for a solution that was simple and effective. She was excited to share that with me. While I was there, Chaplain Corey dropped by to give Mom a hug and a prayer.

Susan came by to see if Mom wanted to join in the balloon toss. When we returned to the room, I could tell Mom was tired. While we were out, Marcia had straightened up the room. Soft music was playing, and Mom's recliner looked cozy, draped with a soft blanket. Marcia moved Mom from her wheelchair to the recliner, and when I left, Mom was dozing comfortably.

Lord, thank You for providing this safe and comfortable environment where my mother is surrounded by those who truly care about her.

KRISTY DEWBERRY

No Assumptions

All the people shall hear and fear and not
act presumptuously again.
—DEUTERONOMY 17:13 (ESV)

I lost count of how many doctors we took Mom to see that year. So many that she was beginning to lose heart. Her newest doctor, a neurologist, gave us a diagnosis at last—parkinsonism. He started Mom on medication and ordered physical therapy with her home-health nurse.

Three months had passed when one day Mom said, "I need new glasses. Again! I don't know what's going on with my eyes."

"Well, when I googled parkinsonism, I found that vision changes are a common symptom," I said casually. It's hard to describe the look that came across Mom's face. Shock, maybe? Sadness? Relief? I wasn't sure. She started to cry. Her tears came slowly at first, then in a great deluge.

"I thought the doctor made up that diagnosis," she said between sobs. "I thought everyone gave up on me and just made up some disease to keep me quiet."

Her words took my breath away. I felt horrible. All this time and I'd mistakenly assumed Mom understood everything. She had always been so sharp and not at all shy about speaking up.

"Why didn't you say anything? I am so sorry. Please forgive me."

I pulled out my phone and tapped a few keys. "Let's clear this up. Parkinsonism is a form of Parkinson's. It affects people differently," I began.

Lord, please remind me not to make assumptions about
what is and isn't clear to my loved one on this journey.
PAMELA HASKIN

Empathy

Rejoice with those who rejoice, and weep with those who weep.
—ROMANS 12:15 (NKJV)

Although Mom liked her new apartment in the assisted living complex, she complained about every little thing. They overcooked the broccoli. The managers were never around when she needed them. Her tablemates didn't speak up, even though they knew she was hard of hearing.

I tried to convince Mom to see these issues from others' points of view. But the more I reasoned, the more frequent her complaints grew. I was weary. Mom was frustrated. *Lord, help me understand Mom better,* I prayed. *My idea isn't working. I need one of Yours.*

A few weeks later, our caregivers' support group leader showed a cartoon: Turtle had fallen into a pit. His friend Bear shouted clichés to him from above, trying to help, but Turtle sank lower in despair. But when Bear climbed into the pit and just sat beside his friend, saying how sorry he was for this dilemma, Turtle brightened. Together they found a way out.

There was my answer—empathy. Mom didn't need advice or explanations. She needed me to identify with her feelings. If I could show her I understood, perhaps she'd be a bit happier, even if the situation never changed.

Next time Mom whined about broccoli or insensitive people, I said, "That is so hard for you. I'd be frustrated too." She nodded, a sad look in her eyes. I wasn't surprised when she changed the subject, smiling once again. God's idea worked.

Dear Lord, help me to grow in empathy so that
my loved ones feel understood.
JEANETTE LEVELLIE

Let's Get Creative

Be glad; rejoice forever in my creation.
—ISAIAH 65:18 (TLB)

We were desperate. Dad had been busy all his life as a farmer and factory worker. Even in retirement, he tended two huge gardens and a fruit orchard. This was not a guy meant to be inactive. Yet that was his reality. Sitting. Watching television. Waiting for my sister or brother or me to come and break the boredom. Waiting for one of the nurses' aides to show up. Going stir-crazy.

Then I found a possibility. In a corner of a store, I spied art kits with no paint to spill. They included felt markers and preprinted pictures. They didn't pretend to be fine art. Still, the pictures were very familiar to Dad: deer or squirrels or farm scenes or a forest. It was worth a try.

To our surprise and delight, he loved them. Those projects filled several hours in his long days, and he'd wake up talking about how he planned to shade in a tree or put highlights on an animal. A neighbor made frames. Now Dad even had gifts he could give.

The person you're caring for may not enjoy art, so try something else. Try asking for a story to record or a recipe to share with the next generation or a song remembered from childhood. Our Creator built into our hearts the need to create. Look for what will work for your loved one.

Thank You, Father, for creating beauty around and within us.
SHIRLEY LEONARD

Hands on Hips

Let your gentleness be evident to all. The Lord is near.
—PHILIPPIANS 4:5 (NIV)

Mom stood in the doorway with her characteristic hands on hips." I read these words in my daughter's short story with some surprise. But, come to think of it, I did have this habit—a way of communicating, "I'm a no-nonsense mom."

Now, with my mother living with us, was I also a no-nonsense daughter? Due to her physical frailties and mild dementia, I laid out my mother's clothes each morning, made sure she swallowed her pills, and on nice days suggested she trade out her favorite word search for a walk to the mailbox and back.

Just how she felt about this role reversal was exposed at a women's retreat. Late the first evening, I said, "Mom, it's bedtime. Why don't you go to your bedroom and start getting ready? I'll come and check on you in a few minutes."

She got out of the rocking chair, rose to her feet, saluted me, and blurted, "Aye, aye, Captain!"

Laughter erupted. I felt both humiliated and humbled. Her words revealed the truth.

In that moment, I knew that I needed God's grace to maintain kindness in my attitude. No more hands on hips. Yes, my support of Mom meant some control of her time, diet, and wardrobe, but my best care would show itself with a humble heart.

Lord, remind me to be as gentle with others as You are with me.
JUDY PALPANT

Sweet Refuge

Taste and see that the LORD is good; blessed is the
one who takes refuge in him.
—PSALM 34:8 (NIV)

I'm just not hungry," my mother-in-law said. The chemotherapy
and radiation had taken its toll on her taste buds and appetite. Food
had always been one of her great joys in life. Whenever she visited, we
chose restaurants serving the things she loved most: liver and onions,
layered desserts, casseroles.

Our family gathered at her favorite restaurant. We'd ordered a
smorgasbord of food options, but nothing looked good to her, although
she wanted to soak in the meal and spend time with us. We picked
out several desserts, hoping something would taste good. The
cheesecakes weren't appealing, and neither was the apple pie. And then
it happened. The waitress brought out strawberry shortcake with giant
sugared biscuits, macerated strawberries dripping with sugar, vanilla
ice cream, and whipped cream.

"I want some of that," my mother-in-law announced.

I leaned over with a tiny bit of everything perched on a spoon,
watching as the sweet summer dessert hit her tongue. She gave
me a big smile. Although it was only a single bite, she found joy in
rediscovering her love of food.

*Lord, help me remember sweet memories and ways You offer
refuge when it seems like there is nowhere to turn.*

AMY BARNES

Asking for Help

"Ask and it will be given to you; seek and you will find;
knock and the door will be opened to you."
—MATTHEW 7:7 (NIV)

I pulled two housedresses from Mom's closet. "Which one?" I
asked her.

"The red one." I slipped the dress over her head. I brushed her hair
and put a little blush on her cheeks. Then I settled her into her chair in
the living room while I went back to start a load of laundry.

"Someone's here!" Mom called.

"Hello!" Vicki, a longtime friend, sang as she let herself in. She
visited with Mom a little while before pulling me aside.

"She's getting worse. Is there anything I can do to help?"

"You are so sweet to offer, but really we're fine." The truth was
we were not fine. Mom needed more and more help. I had to go back
home in a few days. My brother and his wife, both teachers, had to
be at work early every morning. The three of us had been praying for
help. Could Vicki be God's way of helping us?

"Actually, we do need help," I finally admitted. Vicki volunteered
to stop by every weekday morning to help Mom get dressed and ready
for the day. She also ran occasional errands and took Mom to doctor
appointments when we couldn't.

Lord, help me be brave enough to ask for help
and humble enough to accept it.
PAMELA HASKIN

Not a Dirty Word

Where does my help come from? My help comes from the Lord.
—PSALM 121:1–2 (NIV)

M om sat at the table trying to regain her strength. The walk from the living room had taken all her energy. She insisted on having lunch in the kitchen, even though the exertion ruined her appetite every time.

We needed help from hospice. When I suggested it, Mom reacted as if I'd said a dirty word. To her, hospice meant giving up. To me, hospice meant quality-of-life care, for her as a patient and me as a caregiver. I tried to explain the difference, but Mom refused to listen.

At her next appointment, the doctor told her, "You're not knocking on death's door, but it's time for hospice." To my surprise—and relief—she agreed.

A hospice caseworker described the care Mom would receive and said she would actually feel better and enjoy each day more. She assured us that many patients receive services for months, even years. This wasn't "the end."

The next day, Mom's hospice nurse visited. She took interest in Mom as a person, not just as a patient. She pampered her, listened to her, and made her feel special. Mom said, "You are an angel from heaven sent just for me." *And me*, I silently added. The nurse would now make decisions about Mom's health and safety that I wasn't equipped to make. Hospice took care of us both.

*Father, please equip me with the wisdom, heart, and resources
to take care of my loved one as well as myself.*
KAREN SARGENT

No Need to Go It Alone

You shall increase my greatness, and comfort me on every side.
—PSALM 71:21 (NKJV)

Mother was settled in her new apartment, but it was still going to be tough to keep her living independently. She'd given up driving, which meant that getting groceries, running errands, and getting to doctor appointments were going to be a challenge. I was working full-time, as was my husband.

My sons were both away at college. I couldn't do it alone. I wasn't sure where to turn. I discussed my dilemma with a good friend who'd walked the same road. "Sharon, have you called the area Agency on Aging yet? They have lots of services you may not be aware of."

The Agency on Aging was a godsend. They signed Mom up for Meals on Wheels. Arrangements were made for a public health nurse to regularly set up her medications and check her vital signs. Best of all, the caseworker promised to plead Mom's case to the Medicaid waiver program. The waiver program was designed to keep frail elderly people independent—and out of nursing homes—by providing home helpers. The helpers would assist with housework, cooking, and errands and provide companionship in the meantime. There was usually a 2-year waiting list, but the caseworker promised to do her best to get Mom's name moved up on the list.

I breathed a sigh of relief. It takes others to help out sometimes. God doesn't mean for us to go it alone.

Father God, thank You for giving me the strength and humility
to ask for help with caregiving when I need it.
SHARON DRACH MANGAS

Sunlight

For with God nothing shall be impossible.
—LUKE 1:37 (KJV)

Mom's eyesight was deteriorating from macular degeneration, but I didn't know how bad it had gotten until one morning I watched her stoop to pick up something off the floor. She grabbed at it, then studied her empty thumb and forefinger with a puzzled expression. Frowning, she turned to me. Behind the thick lenses of her glasses, her blue-green eyes clouded with concern.

"Mom," I said, "it's just a patch of sunlight."

Over the past several years, we had equipped Mom's in-law apartment with special low-vision aids such as extra halogen lighting, a high-tech magnifying monitor for reading, and big-print phones. Thank the Lord, she could still drive.

And then came the words I think we both had been silently dreading: "I—I don't think I should be driving anymore," she said. Boom. Just like that, our worlds collapsed.

"It's OK, Mom," I said. "Don't worry. We'll work it out."

But I was worried. If Mom no longer drives, who's going to take her to the grocery store? To doctor appointments? To Bible study? To visit her friends? My life was busier than ever with two active teenagers, work, and managing my own household. How was I ever going to meet my mother's needs? My eyes fell on that glimmering patch of sunlight on the floor, a reminder of God's infinite capacity in the most worrisome times. Yes, we would work it out with God's help.

Dear God, help me remember that with You, all things are possible.
KITTY SLATTERY

The Ministry of the Cookie Lady

How sweet are your words to my taste, sweeter
than honey to my mouth!
—PSALM 119:103 (NIV)

My wife, Sandra, and I were caring for Florence, my mother-in-law. I was feeling helpless and frustrated about how to lift Florence out of her increasing depression.

I knew Florence loved baking. So did I. She was known in town as the Cookie Lady, even featured in the local newspaper. She personally delivered her batches of cookies to nursing homes, to children's hospitals, to small businesses, to neighbors, and to shut-ins. But advanced macular degeneration and increasing dementia had robbed her of the ability to maneuver well in the kitchen.

I got an idea. I asked Florence to show me how to make her favorite cookie recipe. She was hesitant but brightened at the suggestion. I assured her I would serve as her sous-chef and help her. We struggled a bit with baking soda versus baking powder, but we finished our prep.

As we pulled out the first batch and savored the rich snickerdoodle, Florence started crying. *Great*, I thought, *this was supposed to cheer her up.* "We forgot something," she wailed. I double-checked the recipe. Nope, everything was in that cookie. "I didn't say a prayer before I put the cookies in the oven," she said. "And I don't know who these cookies are for."

I took in a ragged breath and said, "They're for me."

For Florence, each batch of cookies was her own personal ministry—an expression of her heart given freely.

*Lord, help me give freely to others around me today,
making a difference in their day.*
TERRY CLIFTON

When the Sun Goes Down

Love bears all things, believes all things,
hopes all things, endures all things.
—1 CORINTHIANS 13:7 (ESV)

The sun was dipping lower in the graying sky. It was almost 6:15 p.m., and Mom was taking a brief evening nap on her couch. It was a rare respite from taking care of her, and I knew that at any moment she could awaken. I heard her stir and knew it was the dreaded time of day when the sundowning would begin, a terrible side of Alzheimer's.

"Where have you been?" Mom said confrontationally. "You haven't been here for 3 days!"

Never mind the fact that I had been with her the last 6 hours. Sundowning syndrome had robbed her of the day's earlier memories.

"Now, Mom, that's not true. I've been here all day," I told her.

"No, you haven't!" she screamed.

I kept my expression calm and resisted the urge to disagree with her. After all, I knew better. The books I had borrowed from the Alzheimer's Association stated not to argue because it would only upset the person. I took a deep breath. "Well, I'm here now," I said in a soothing voice. "Would you like to go sit outside?"

As I helped her down the front porch steps, I could tell she had no idea she was even at her own house. Her eyes had fogged over, and she was lost in her own mind. It must have been so scary for her. It was scary for me, too, but at least I could control my anguish when she couldn't.

Lord, help me remember to take a deep breath of calm
whenever the duties of caregiving take a hard turn.
JEANNIE HUGHES

The Power of Presence

Whatever you do, do it heartily, as to the Lord.
—COLOSSIANS 3:23 (NKJV)

I finished up a long work shift, exhausted, but I still wanted to visit my dad at his care facility. On the way there, I stopped at a gas station to grab some of Dad's favorite treats: sunflower seeds, Jolly Ranchers, ginger ale.

"Here, I brought you something," I said, holding out the bag to him. As my dad took out each item, he held it high, saying, "Oh, I love these," and "Can you help me open this?" He offered to share, but I wanted him to save them.

I'd already been gone from home for over 12 hours, so I knew I couldn't stay long. "I better get going," I told him after an hour.

"Oh, but let me just show you this one cool video I found," was my dad's answer. One video became two, became four, but I couldn't make myself pull away. He was clearly enjoying our time together.

Finally, I looked at the clock—8:30 p.m.—and gently touched Dad's hand. "I really do have to go. I'll come back tomorrow." I hugged him, sorry to leave. It was hard, but I knew I'd be back the next day, and that was what mattered.

Lord, help me remember how important the gift of presence is.
MONICA HERALD

Avoid Regrets

*Love is patient and kind. Love is not jealous or boastful
or proud or rude. It does not demand its own way. It is not
irritable, and it keeps no record of being wronged.*
—1 CORINTHIANS 13:4–5 (NLT)

Everybody has regrets after a loved one has passed away; words they should have said and those they wish they could take back. Alzheimer's is a different type of death. It's a death of the mind, not the body.

At first, Mom's Alzheimer's progressed slowly. I thought I still had time to express love and gratitude. But suddenly Mom was no longer Mom. I don't know the exact moment I lost her. One day she knew me, and then one day she didn't.

I always had a hard time expressing love to my mother. I don't know why. The words just stuck in my throat. Maybe because Mom declared her love to me so often and effusively that it made me feel awkward and uncomfortable. Yet she never gave up on me. She was always hopeful that the words would come more easily to me and that I would reciprocate her words of love.

Now that she no longer expresses her love, I long for those words. I tell her that I love her every single time I visit, in hopes that she somehow knows who I am and understands that I am finally reciprocating. But I'm afraid the opportunity has passed.

Express gratitude and love every chance you get. Tomorrow may be too late.

*Lord, each moment I have with my loved one is precious.
Let me not miss a single opportunity to right a wrong or
to express my love and gratitude.*
KRISTY DEWBERRY

The Talk

Cast all your anxiety on him because he cares for you.
—1 PETER 5:7 (NIV)

Oh, that dreaded nursing home talk. When do you have it? Is it giving up? Is it the right thing to do? Those were the questions my brother Steve and I asked each other when we found ourselves nearing that time with our mother. She could no longer walk or help much in her own care. The doctor said Mom would soon need around-the-clock skilled nursing care.

We expected Mom would not agree to moving at first, but we hoped she would once she got used to the idea. In truth, she was rapidly reaching a point when we would have to make her move. So, united in prayer and love for her, Steve and I broached the subject with Mom.

"Y'all just want to put me in there to die!" she snapped. Tears brimmed in her eyes.

Her words stung. I fell to my knees in front of her and took her hands in mine. "This will be one of the hardest things we will ever have to do. We will not leave you out of the decision-making, but you do need to start thinking about it," I said.

Some weeks after that, Mom agreeably, if somewhat reluctantly, moved into a nursing home. It was the right thing to do for her—no matter how bad it felt to us as her children.

*Lord, please continue to grant us wisdom as we make
our way through difficult decisions ahead.*
PAMELA HASKIN

Helping the Pain Go Away

Good people are kind to their animals.
—PROVERBS 12:10 (CEV)

Mom had plastered the inside of her front door with greeting cards featuring kitties. Photos of her beloved cat, Rufus, covered her fridge door. "Do you ever hear from the family who adopted Rufus, Mom?"

"Just at Christmastime. Look at this picture they sent me of him sprawled under their tree!" Although she chuckled, I knew the cards and pictures were little compensation for the Rufus-shaped hole in her heart.

Mom had always treated the huge six-toed tabby like a grandchild. Spoiling him with treats. Talking baby talk to him. Fretting when he escaped outdoors. When she moved from California to Illinois, she made the painful decision to leave Rufus behind. She'd realized that caring for a cat had become too much for her, although it was another month before she was actually diagnosed with Alzheimer's.

A couple with plenty of land and well-mannered children adopted Rufus. "I'm so relieved he'll have a loving family," Mom said. But the sadness in her voice was unmistakable.

I couldn't take Mom's pain away. But I could have her over for Sunday dinner, where she petted and chatted with my two cats, one a Rufus look-alike. I made sure her Mother's Day and birthday cards featured kittens, so she could add to her collection. Mostly I prayed for Mom. Better than anyone, Jesus understands the pain of goodbyes.

Lord, thank You for understanding our pain. When faced with difficult decisions, may we find Your wisdom and grace.
JEANETTE LEVELLIE

Knitting Happiness

See, I am doing a new thing! Now it springs up;
do you not perceive it?
—ISAIAH 43:19 (NIV)

About 35 years ago, my mother started a family tradition. For the arrival of her first grandchild, my mom knitted a lovely Christmas stocking. It was a big hit and a very special gift. Two years later, a second grandchild arrived, and Mom took out her knitting needles again.

When one of my cousins had his first child, Mom got busy with the yarn. Then another cousin had a baby, and another, and yet another. Mom's knitting needles saw a lot of activity through the years. She crafted more than forty-five Christmas stockings to give to the new members of our growing family tree.

But when she was diagnosed with progressive supranuclear palsy—a serious neurological disease—among the first to be affected were her fine motor skills, like those needed to knit. She just wasn't able to do it anymore.

But the stork continued to make regular deliveries. So I decided to pick up the gauntlet, er, the needles. Mom had taught me how to knit when I was a kid. Although I didn't knit as well as she did, I studied the patterns and have continued her tradition. So far, I've made a dozen or so stockings and hope to make many more.

Mom passed away in 2008. And still I continue to knit Christmas stockings. After all, some traditions are worth preserving through love and care.

Lord, thank You for reminding me of my loved one's
traditions to pass on.
MARYANNE CURRAN

In Her Defense

Be kind and compassionate to one another, forgiving
each other, just as in Christ God forgave you.
—EPHESIANS 4:32 (NIV)

I patted my mother's back. "I'm sorry. I didn't mean to yell. Please don't cry."

Frustration had gotten the better of me. My words may not have been harsh, but my tone was. I felt awful. In my mind, excuses pinged like a game of pinball, with lights flashing and flippers clicking. I was tired. I was making dinner. It was the third time she'd called for me in the last 5 minutes. They were all valid excuses for me to be annoyed but still not good enough to justify my behavior.

I recalled how, as a child, I would shout, "Ma, come here! Hurry!" A minute later, I'd be calling again. Patience was far from my understanding. After all, I was young.

I remembered how my mother would say, "Give me a minute. I only have two hands." But it was never mean enough to wrench tears from my eyes.

I don't recall who said it to me that day, but it was as jarring as a bolt of electricity. They were words I'd never forget: "It must be hard for her, becoming so dependent."

Bells sounded. Scriptures flashed. I repented. I would give her ice cream for dessert.

I knew God forgave me, and so did my mother. Now I would work on forgiving myself.

Lord, help me to be compassionate so that
I may receive that same compassion.
PAMELA HIRSON

Opening

Hatred stirs up strife, but love covers all offenses.
—PROVERBS 10:12 (RSV)

My father looked smaller than before, sitting on his hospital bed, his hair unkempt, his face unshaven. I sat on a sofa several feet away from him, enshrouded in a yellow hospital paper gown, gloved and masked, precautions taken to protect me from his MRSA infection. But more than anything, I kept my heart protected—from him. We'd never had a good relationship. We'd been in this cycle for 9 months now: hospital, rehab, home; repeat. I was exhausted by it all.

"Do you remember Ollie?" he asked suddenly out of nowhere, his voice weak. His question surprised me.

"I do," I answered. Every so often, we'd go to the park and a tree would "talk" to me, but it only happened when my dad and I were together. The tree's name was Ollie.

"You loved Ollie the tree." Dad smiled, clearly transported back in time, remembering a 7-year-old me, sitting next to the tree.

"I was sad when I'd go by myself and he wouldn't talk to me," I told my father. "The only times he did, telling me about his adventures with the other trees, were when I was with you." I smiled and leaned toward him. "You were Ollie, weren't you?"

My dad grinned but didn't answer my question. "I'm so happy you're here. It really means a lot to me."

"I'm glad I came too, Dad." I walked over to his bed and squeezed his hand through my gloves.

Lord, help me with the ongoing work of opening my heart to my loved ones, even when the past has been painful.
MONICA HERALD

A Memorable Birthday

Can a woman forget her nursing child . . . ?
Even these may forget, but I won't forget you.
—ISAIAH 49:15 (CEB)

Veterans Day 1948 proved to be memorable for Mom—my birth, her firstborn. Record snows that year meant treacherous roads. Dad missed my arrival while coaching his high school basketball team's out-of-town game.

Exactly 5 years later to the day, my sister was born. To my young mind, it was just as I'd expected. After all, I did ask for a baby sister for my birthday. Over the years our birthday photos showed the two of us wearing matching dresses with a two-tiered cake—a large bottom layer with a smaller one on top. One year we wore necklaces with the numbers "5" and "10" hung in silver around our respective necks.

In her later years, Mom's dementia robbed her of these memories. She no longer remembered our November 11 birthdays. While not surprising, it still brought sadness to our hearts and to hers when we reminded her.

In her 96th year, I went down the stairs on my birthday to make sure she was awake. Dread dogged my steps, knowing that I would again have to tell Mom that it was my birthday. I opened the door, and there she stood wearing her lavender robe and a big smile. With arms wide open, she exclaimed, "Happy birthday, Daughter!"

Wrapped in her embrace, I felt a great sense of well-being sweep over me. That moment redeemed all the previous years, eaten by the locust of dementia.

Thank You, Lord, for the comfort of being
remembered—especially by You.
JUDY PALPANT

Lost and Found

I will search for the lost and bring back the strays.
I will bind up the injured and strengthen the weak.
—EZEKIEL 34:16 (NIV)

Where's the coffeepot?" my husband, David, asked as he opened and closed the cabinet doors. His morning task since his mother, Stevie, had moved in with us 3 years ago was to make her coffee. Stevie's Alzheimer's had progressed to the point that the family had decided she shouldn't live alone.

"I don't know," I said. While living with us, Stevie believed she was on vacation and would only be staying with us for "a little visit." She also believed that everything had a place, and if she felt an item was out of place, she found a home for it.

The word *where* began most sentences in our home after Stevie moved in. "Mom, where's my math book?" "Mom, where are my shoes?" "Where's the bath mat?" Question after question about misplaced items. I prayed for so many lost things to be found. And if not, I prayed the disappointed one would be able to let it go. Sometimes the disappointed one was me.

We learned how to adjust and adapt as a family. At times that meant making coffee in a large measuring cup. That day, I finally found the coffeepot in the bottom drawer of the refrigerator next to the carrots.

Father, though things may go missing—coffeepots or
even memories—I know I am never lost to You.
EDWINA PERKINS

Tough Love

Do everything in love.
—1 CORINTHIANS 16:14 (NIV)

I hid Mom's medicine organizer, hoping she wouldn't notice it missing from the table beside her recliner. But she did.

"Where's my medicine?" She searched around her chair. Mom was obsessed with the little pills that filled each box. She would open the morning container and count them, then repeat the counting at lunch, in the afternoon, and in the evening. She continually asked if it was time to take her medicine.

I inherited my mom's patience, so I would watch her count and remind her what time she'd take her next dose. One evening I found a pill she had dropped on the floor, and then another, which meant she hadn't taken them. Then she took a dose only an hour after the previous one. I knew how upset she would be, but I had to move her medicine. As a mother of teen girls, I was used to measuring how much independence to allow my daughters. As the daughter of an aging parent, I would never get used to taking independence away.

"Mom, I have your medicine." I gently explained why, aggrieved by the defeated look on her face.

I changed the subject. "It's time for dinner. I made soup." Mom had hardly eaten all week. I hoped she would be tempted. "Would you like a bowl?"

She thought for a moment. "I want ice cream."

I patted her arm. "Ice cream it is."

Father, as I care for my loved ones, help me always
remember to honor them with dignity.
KAREN SARGENT

Monday Night Dancing

"I will refresh the weary and satisfy the faint."
—JEREMIAH 31:25 (NIV)

Although we lived hundreds of miles apart, Mom and I found one way we could still be together and enjoy each other's company. For a couple of hours on Monday nights, we would forget about the battle with Parkinson's that kept Mom homebound far away. I could even forget about the guilt that sometimes plagued me for not being able to see her as often as we both would have liked.

Our evenings together began when the host announced each celebrity and their professional partner on *Dancing with the Stars*. During the string of commercials between each dance routine, I'd call Mom. In my mind, I could see her fumbling to answer the phone with her gnarled hands.

"Do you have a favorite yet?" she always asked even before saying hello.

"Not yet. Do you?"

We talked about purple sequins and feathery dresses, foxtrots, jives, and tangos. We usually agreed on our favorite choices but often disagreed with the judges. Then, suddenly, one of us would shout, "The show's back on!" and we hung up quickly, sometimes mid-sentence. We didn't want to miss a second of the next dance.

It felt to me as if Mom and I were actually together in the same room on those wonderful Monday evenings. She always seemed more energized and cheerful after sharing a night of dance. I was too.

Thank You, Lord, for giving us ways to spend time together even when we're apart from our loved ones. Thank You for refreshing both of our spirits in such a beautiful way.

PAMELA HASKIN

The Commander

This service that you perform is not only supplying
the needs of the Lord's people but is also overflowing
in many expressions of thanks to God.
—2 CORINTHIANS 9:12 (NIV)

My wife, Sandra, and I were living in her folks' basement as their personal caregivers. Her mother had fallen and suffered a series of ministrokes. Sandra's stepfather, Dale, a retired army career officer, was also dealing with increasing cognitive challenges.

One morning I woke up to Dale standing at the foot of our bed. "I have a request," he said in his formidable military commander voice. He suddenly pulled a small knife from behind his back. I got up in a flash, with no idea why he was brandishing a weapon.

"My toenails need cutting!" he said. "Your mother-in-law uses this knife on all her vegetables. It should help you complete your task."

I realized that my father-in-law, the commander, was not out to frighten me or gross me out with the thought of repurposing a knife used for our meals. His soft, pleading eyes revealed a cry for help. It was at that moment that I saw beyond Dale, the commander. He was an elderly soldier reaching out for help from a member of the troop, the caregiver.

"It will be my honor, sir," I whispered.

Later that morning, with actual nail clippers in hand, I began a weekly routine with Dale. We had both entered a new chapter in our son-in-law and father-in-law book of caregiving.

Dear Lord, help me be sensitive to those I love
and better able to discern their needs.
TERRY CLIFTON

Angels Among Us

He will command his angels concerning you
to guard you in all your ways.
—PSALM 91:11 (NIV)

My mother was a strong woman, proud and fiercely independent. Despite her blindness from age-related macular degeneration, she was reluctant to ask for help—even from me. And the idea of being visited by a professional caregiver—an "outsider"—was out of the question! Home-care aides were for old, sick people. Not Mom.

"I'm not sick," she declared, stubbornly shaking her head. "I just can't see."

But with each passing day, it was clear Mom did need outside help. One afternoon, inspiration struck.

"Mom," I said, "I just had the most wonderful idea. How would you like to have a personal assistant? You know, someone to help you keep up with correspondence, do errands, that sort of thing."

"Personal assistant?" Mom's eyes lit up with delight. "Why, yes. I like that idea!"

Through an agency called Home Instead, Mom interviewed and hired a cheerful, energetic aide named Debbie, who came two mornings a week to help her with her mail, sort photos, do small household tasks, and run local errands. Over time, the two women grew very close—so close that Mom affectionately called Debbie "my angel."

Truth be told, Debbie was my angel too.

Thank You, God, for sending Your caring
angels—heavenly and human!
KITTY SLATTERY

The Beauty in Routine

Give us each day our daily bread.
—LUKE 11:3 (NIV)

When I began to make more frequent trips to visit my parents who lived two states away, I was very task-oriented. I planned to clean, shop for groceries, and prepare a freezer full of meals. But each time I got ready to run errands, my parents wanted to go with me—and they'd set the itinerary. We'd first stop at Steak 'n Shake, where the waitresses knew their names and regular orders. Then we'd head to Walmart, where my dad would park himself on a bench near the checkout, and my mom would drive a cart. As my mom zipped through the store, I'd hurriedly throw my groceries into her cart, trying to keep up. Then my dad would meet us at the cash register to pay. This happened multiple times until their routine became mine.

A year later, when it was time to move my parents into assisted living near me, the transition was extremely difficult. But it didn't take long before we found a Steak 'n Shake nearby and met a favorite waiter who remembered us and our orders. And a Walmart where my mom could drive a cart and my dad could wait on a bench. The routine that had frustrated me in the beginning had now become a saving grace, a way to ease the pain during a time of transition.

Lord, thank You for Your tender mercies and our daily routines.
MISSY TIPPENS

Celebration

His anger is but for a moment, and his favor is for
a lifetime. Weeping may tarry for the night,
but joy comes with the morning.
—PSALM 30:5 (ESV)

My mother-in-law loved every holiday and celebrated with sparkle and Pinterest-worthy decorations. Her Stage 4 pancreatic cancer meant we would have only one more of each holiday with her. One more set of birthdays. One more Easter, Thanksgiving, Christmas.

That last Christmas came. She was homebound, wearing a mask to protect her from germs. We arrived with masks on and gifts. Simple gifts: books, magazines, framed school pictures of the kids.

The recent chemo trips had left her with no energy to get holiday decorations out of the attic. No tree and no lights, no angels or Santas. Christmas cards sat unopened in the kitchen.

My husband and I headed out to shop for Christmas decorations. It was Christmas Eve, and I didn't expect to find many holiday options at stores. The shelves were nearly bare except for some lights and tinsel. One Charlie Brown tree sat next to the garden-aisle fertilizer. We bought everything they had.

While my mother-in-law slept, my husband, the kids, and I hung strands of lights and filled in the bare spots of the tiny tree with butterfly ornaments. When she woke up, it was Christmas morning, and we had a tree and gifts and a celebration. There was new joy in the holiday morning!

Lord, help us celebrate Your love and joy in
whatever moments we can find them.
AMY BARNES

In God's Hands

"For I know the plans I have for you," declares the LORD,
"plans to prosper you and not to harm you,
plans to give you hope and a future."
—JEREMIAH 29:11 (NIV)

I put my head down on the steering wheel. A flat tire? Really? I was picking up a pizza for Mom. She rarely cooked anymore. I called AAA and then let Mom know it would be a while.

Driving back and forth to Indianapolis every weekend to see her was taking a toll on me. It wasn't sustainable. It was time to have a conversation with Mom about moving.

After her heart catheter procedure, her cardiologist threw out a lot of medical terms, but the one that stuck with me was "heart failure." Even with medication, her energy level was never going to be the same. She needed help to continue living independently.

Over lunch, I broached the subject. Mom took it in quietly. After a long pause, she told me she knew it was probably for the best. She had raised three children on her own after my father's untimely death over 60 years ago, and she was nothing if not resilient.

We made a plan. I'd check into senior housing for her, and she'd call her apartment complex to see if she could get out of her lease early.

In many ways, my role as a caregiver was only just beginning. But after all the years she had looked after me, it was the least I could do.

Lord, when hard decisions loom, we turn to You. We rest
in the knowledge that our welfare is in Your hands.
SHARON DRACH MANGAS

A Day of Pampering

Even to your old age I am he, and to gray hairs I will carry you.
—ISAIAH 46:4 (ESV)

Holding tight to my mother, I carefully helped her out of the shower. I had bathed her and washed her hair. Rubbing lotion on her back was followed by blow-drying and curling her thinning hair.

"I hope they pay you well. You have a terrible job," Mom said. It had been several months since she recognized me as her daughter. Alzheimer's had taken her memories. She no longer remembered the endless card games we played when I was younger. No memory of quizzing me on spelling words or checking my papers for accurate grammar.

"Don't you look pretty?" I told her, smoothing rouge on to her cheeks and brushing her face with powder.

"Oh, you're just saying that to be kind," she said.

But she did look pretty. Her eyes were still a vibrant blue, and all done up, she looked much younger than her 86 years. She smiled up at me; Alzheimer's had not yet robbed her of the ability to show expression.

I filed each nail and finished it off with a clear coat of polish. Mom loved being pampered and shown extra attention. Although the work was tiring, I felt good about being the one who could make her feel special. It made me feel special too.

Lord, thank You for giving me opportunities to make
those in my care feel especially beloved.
JEANNIE HUGHES

When We Grow Weary

*He gives strength to the weary and increases
the power of the weak.*

—ISAIAH 40:29 (NIV)

Watching Parkinson's destroy my mother's body was brutal. I wanted her to fight harder. It seemed she was giving up.

"I don't like to exercise. Besides, it doesn't really help," Mom said.

"I'll do it with you," I said, determined not to give in to her arguments, even though I didn't like exercising either. I picked up two elastic bands Mom's therapist had left behind. I handed one to Mom. "Show me what you're supposed to do."

Mom gave in with a huff, scooted to the edge of her chair and put the band under her foot. "You kind of march in place with it," she said.

"Try holding more resistance against the band. Do it slower like this," I said, copying her movements.

She tried again. "If I do it the way you and the therapist insist on, I still don't like it."

"Neither do I. A slow five more! One, two, three . . ." The elastic band suddenly slipped off my foot and bounced up, hitting me in the face.

Mom started laughing. "Not that slow!"

We did every exercise on her list. Mom was spent and ready for a nap by the time we finished. I knew I would have sore muscles the next morning, but it was fun for both of us when we took on the task together.

*Lord, when we become weary from the struggle, remind us
today that You are the one who makes us strong.*

PAMELA HASKIN

Finding Common Ground

Make my joy complete by being like-minded, having
the same love, being one in spirit and of one mind.
—PHILIPPIANS 2:2 (NIV)

My dad and I shared many things: We were fans of the Boston
Celtics, Gene Kelly, and mysteries and thrillers.

As Dad got older, he faced multiple health issues including
diabetes, stroke, and seizures. But what challenged him the most was
losing much of his eyesight due to glaucoma. Because he was legally
blind, he had to give up reading. I felt so sad for him and a little sad
for me, too, because we couldn't talk about the twists and turns in the
latest book we had read.

Luckily, we found a solution. Perkins School for the Blind in
Watertown, Massachusetts, has a books-on-tape library, and it was easy
for me to order tapes for him. When our mailman would deliver the
tapes in our mail slot, they made a distinct thud as they hit the ground.

"I think I got some books," my dad would call out to me after he
heard the familiar sound. "What did you get me?" he'd ask. He was
always so excited—like a kid at Christmas as I read the titles and
authors' names.

I would try to read the same book that Dad was listening to so we
could continue our literary conversations. Those times remain some
of the best I spent with my father.

Finding a hobby you can pursue together or even just sharing
something in common with the person you're taking care of can bring
so much more joy and richness to the relationship.

*Lord, thank You for giving me the joy of common
ground with my loved one.*
MARYANNE CURRAN

Mirror, Mirror

You, LORD, hear the desire of the afflicted; you encourage them, and you listen to their cry.
—PSALM 10:17 (NIV)

Panic gripped my heart as I dug through my purse, frantic over missing keys. "I'm behaving just like Mom," I told my husband, Kevin, anxiously.

"No, you aren't, honey. Everyone loses things." He reminded me of how much I had on my mind lately. Helping Mom. Serving as taxi driver for our three teenage grandkids while our daughter worked. Writing. Speaking. Oh, and my day job.

Yet nothing Kevin said convinced me I wasn't exhibiting the same dementia symptoms I'd noticed in Mom 8 years ago. Symptoms that had only worsened.

A few weeks later, our caregivers' group leader scheduled a speaker from the Alzheimer's Association. Before the meeting, I planned to ask the speaker if my forgetful moments, lost items and confusion were signs of early-onset dementia. But I never got the chance.

Near the end of her talk, she stated matter-of-factly, "It's typical for those who care for Alzheimer's patients to mirror their behaviors. You spend so much time with your loved one, you start acting like them." She reassured us that it doesn't mean we're getting dementia. Only that we are trying to relate to our loved one during this scary time in their lives.

I smiled all the way home. Kev was kind enough not to say, "Told you so."

Dear Lord, thank You for sending the right people
at the right time to answer our hardest questions.
JEANETTE LEVELLIE

Angels on Earth

*Are not all angels ministering spirits sent to serve
those who will inherit salvation?*
—HEBREWS 1:14 (NIV)

I t may be time to get hospice involved," the nurse at Mom's facility
told me.

Wait. What? "But isn't that for people who are about to die? Mom
has Alzheimer's, but physically she's healthier than I am!"

The nurse explained that Mom met the criteria for hospice
because she had experienced some weight loss, even though death
was not imminent.

That was 3 years ago, and hospice is still involved. They come by
two or three times a week to check her vitals, bathe her, and make
sure she is getting the care she needs. Her weight has remained stable
throughout these years.

The hospice chaplain visits weekly. He sometimes plays his guitar,
and they sing hymns together. He calls to update me after his visits,
and we commiserate or laugh together, depending on how the day
went. Our particular hospice will bring gifts, schedule hand massages,
offer pet therapy, and celebrate special occasions.

Hospice workers are truly angels on earth. But I have yet to meet
anybody dealing with Alzheimer's who is aware that this resource
might be available to their loved one. See if your loved one is eligible!

*Lord, thank You for providing hospice care for my mother. What a
blessing it is to have extra help in caring for her and ministering
to her physical, emotional, and spiritual needs.*
KRISTY DEWBERRY

Knowing When to Take Control

Wisdom is found in those who take advice.
—PROVERBS 13:10 (NIV)

My mother-in-law didn't drive great distances. She made two trips a week on country roads within a 3-mile radius of her home. Then she was diagnosed with macular degeneration. As the optometrist explained the disease, I knew her driving days would soon end. I hoped to avoid a battle of wills when that day arrived.

I told the optometrist that when he said she could no longer drive, we would abide by his advice. My mother-in-law looked at me for a moment, then seconded the decision.

Often a caregiver has to take control of another person's life. Independence is the last thing my mother-in-law wanted to relinquish and the last thing I wanted to take from her.

Many other decisions followed this one. For any that involved safety or medical issues, we accepted the advice of the professionals. The less significant ones were left to her. What would you like from the grocery? Do you want to go shopping? Which store? What would you like to do today?

By leaving the small decisions to her, she maintained some control of her own life. But in times when decisions were critical and needed to be made right away, I joined hands with my family and asked God for the wisdom needed.

Dear Heavenly Father, please help me to seek Your wisdom above all else.
KATHY BOYD THOMPSON

On Eagles' Wings

Those who hope in the LORD will renew their strength.
They will soar on wings like eagles; they will run and not
grow weary, they will walk and not be faint.

—ISAIAH 40:31 (NIV)

My mother passed away after 7 years with Alzheimer's. We celebrated her life with a lovely memorial service. While I missed her very much, I had to admit that I also felt relieved. I was glad for rest after 7 years of attending to her many needs.

That rest proved to be short-lived. Only 1 month after my mother's death, my mother-in-law fell seriously ill and had to be hospitalized. Helping my wife care for her mother, I found myself jumping back into my caregiving role. We both did.

I often referred to the verse above, glad that God gives us bursts of strength like soaring on eagles' wings. Thankfully my mother-in-law recovered, but that meant we were resuming our long-term caregiving duties. We needed stamina for the trials ahead.

Crises that soon subside can still be very stressful, and pushing through them can require the ability to run without fatiguing. Chronic stressors—like the challenges of continuously caring for a loved one—can be even harder. Thus, I find hope in asking God not only for short bursts of strength but also for the endurance to keep walking the arduous path day in and day out.

Dear Heavenly Father, thanks for renewing my strength every day.
Help me remember to trust You when I grow weary.

JEFF BJORCK

Gifts

Do not forget to do good and to share with others,
for with such sacrifices God is pleased.
—HEBREWS 13:16 (NIV)

For nearly a year, my mother-in-law lived with us after a series of illnesses prevented her from staying on her own. I had recently retired from teaching, so much of the day I was home alone with Granny. We spent a lot of time watching television or talking about family issues, but beyond the superficial chatter of life, we hadn't bonded over much else.

In the fall, my husband, John, and I were scheduled to work at a spiritual retreat. Many of us involved in the event were preparing snacks for the participants, and I had set aside a day to assemble 130 treat bags. Since it was such a large undertaking, I asked Granny if she'd help me. We arranged the items for the bags between us on the table and settled in to work. As she sat opposite me, we silently prayed for each person who would receive the gift.

Sitting in perfect silence across from my husband's mother, I felt closer to her than ever before. When we finished all the bags, she confided, "I really enjoyed doing something for someone else. It was nice to take my mind off my own problems."

I was also thankful. Thankful for the precious moment I had shared with her as we focused on other people and God's love for them.

Lord, as Saint Francis reminded us, it's in giving that we truly receive.
LORI DURHAM

Feeling Needed

Is not wisdom found among the aged?
Does not long life bring understanding?
—JOB 12:12 (NIV)

I pasted a bright smile on my face as I entered my mother's room at the rehab facility. I couldn't let Mom know how troubled I was about my children. Years before, I'd vowed to share only good news with my parents. Having raised my brothers and me, they deserved a respite from worries about kids.

It was a warm, sunny day, so I wheeled Mom outside into the garden. We exchanged small talk for a while before Mom fixed me with those crystal blue eyes of hers. "What's wrong, honey?" The compassion in her voice undid me, and I burst into tears.

"Oh, Mom, the kids are a mess, and so am I! I'm a terrible mother. I can't seem to get anything done, and the kids don't respect me or obey me."

"Tell me," she encouraged.

So for the next 30 minutes, I shared my tales of woe—broken curfews, bad grades, unsavory boyfriends, dirty rooms, disrespect. Then for the next 5 minutes, Mom gave me advice, all of it spot on, ending with her favorite: "This, too, shall pass."

It was amazing how much better I felt, having poured my heart out to her, but then guilt overwhelmed me. "I'm so sorry for burdening you with my problems."

"Are you kidding, honey?" she said. "This is the first time I've felt needed in months. Thank you for giving me a chance to help."

Lord, help me remember that no matter our age,
we all still want to feel needed.
PAT DYSON

Greetings, Stranger

Love your neighbor as yourself.
—LEVITICUS 19:18 (JPS)

As we walked along the busy city streets, Mom pulled away from me to greet one more person. "Here we go again," I muttered quietly.

"Hello, dear, how are you?" Mom asked a woman in a wide sun hat. She stepped into her path and gave her a big hug.

"Do I know you?" the woman said, clearly startled by the display of affection.

Uh-oh, I thought, *what should I do now?* I didn't want to tell this stranger that Mom had Alzheimer's. By labeling her, I would be limiting the way this woman saw her. Besides, after a few minutes of conversation with Mom, it was usually easy to tell there was something wrong anyway.

"I think we've made a mistake," I finally said, stepping in to take Mom's hand, "but it's a pleasure to meet people with nice smiles."

As a parting gift, Mom gave the woman another hug.

And then we were on our way. I knew it was useless to feel embarrassed. My enthusiastic mother never missed an opportunity to greet someone or say hello. It was as if she was wired to spread joy, and as her Alzheimer's progressed, it seemed that human connection was nearly all she had left.

I couldn't control how Mom interacted with the world, nor did I want to.

Dear God, help me to accept my loved one in all her glory and to find blessings in the ways she still seeks connection.
MIRIAM GREEN

Best in the End

I will rejoice and be glad in your steadfast love, because you
have seen my affliction; you have known the distress of my soul.
—PSALM 31:7 (ESV)

Just between us, let's admit it. Caregiving is a lot of work. The needs of our loved ones can be physically and emotionally exhausting, especially if the caregiving stretches out over a few years. Or, perhaps, you are like me—the guilt-ridden daughter who lived far away from her mother when she needed care. Believe me, the guilt is wearing too.

Though my mother understood I could not be there all the time, she still wanted me there all the time. I went to see her as often as I could, usually every few months. My sister-in-law Missy graciously stepped up to become Mom's primary caregiver. I felt awful about it. "I'm so sorry. I know it should be me taking care of Mom," I often lamented to Missy.

"God prepared me for this," Missy told me. "I went through this with my own mother a few years ago. I know just what to do, and I love your mother." It worked out for the best in the end because Missy did not mind telling Mom what to do and making her do it. The truth was that Mom took it much better coming from Missy than she ever did anything coming from me. One way or another, God arranges everything just right.

Lord, thank You for showing me, time and again,
what is best for both me and my loved one.
PAMELA HASKIN

Cast Your Worries Aside

I can do all this through him who gives me strength.
—PHILIPPIANS 4:13 (NIV)

This time, Dad had gone to the hospital for inexplicable kidney problems and low oxygen levels. With test after test, the doctors had tried to figure out why things were failing. No answers so far, just lots of waiting. He'd already been in the ICU for over 2 weeks when I walked in to find a woman I'd never seen at his bedside. "I'm Elizabeth with palliative care. Your dad made some changes. Can I tell you about them?"

I bit my lip and looked at my father. He seemed lucid and alert tonight, but he looked terrible. His skin was sallow and paper thin, his hands and arms bruised from needles. I took a deep breath and nodded for Elizabeth to go on.

"He's set a limit for ventilation and fluids and chosen to not resuscitate," she told me.

I blinked. I'd been warned, but I wasn't prepared.

"Do you understand?" Elizabeth asked.

"Yes, thank you," I said, and then, just like that, she was gone. I turned to my dad and asked, "Do you want to talk about it?"

"Not really," he said. "I'm reading a new mystery today. Wanna hear?"

"Sure," I said. Now wasn't the time to push the conversation; there'd be time enough tomorrow. So I moved my chair closer and listened to him tell me the story.

Father, help me remember to set my worries aside, trusting that You will be with me when I have to pick them back up.

MONICA HERALD

Remembering Beauty

The LORD is close to the brokenhearted and saves
those who are crushed in spirit.
—PSALM 34:18 (NIV)

I had never seen my mom's spirit so broken as I did after she went through a mastectomy for breast cancer. I tried to care for her and be strong, but her sadness hurt my heart.

A week after the surgery, I marched into her room and informed her we were going out.

"I don't want to," she said.

"I know. That's why I made an appointment."

She raised her brow. "For what?"

"We're scheduled for mother-daughter pictures." Before she could protest, I continued, "I'm doing your makeup, I've already picked out our outfits, and we have to be there in 2 hours." Mom never wore much makeup, but she allowed me to give her a complete makeover that day.

At the studio, the photographer couldn't believe Mom had had surgery so recently and kept telling her how good she looked. On the way home, we talked and laughed about the fun we'd had in our photo session. It was the first time Mom had laughed since her surgery.

Those pictures with Mom are my favorite ones of her because the photographer captured her gentle yet fighting spirit. He also captured her beauty, something she needed to be reminded she still had.

Father, help me to show others there can be beauty even in hard times.
EDWINA PERKINS

Sprinkles of Love

*"My grace is sufficient for you, for my power is
made perfect in weakness."*
—2 CORINTHIANS 12:9 (NIV)

As Daddy's 74th birthday neared, I knew he would not live to celebrate another year, so I wanted this birthday to be special. He had always loved his mother's caramel icing, so I secretly called my aunt for the recipe. The perfect birthday surprise!

Cooking is not one of my talents, but how hard could it be? I gathered ingredients and followed directions: cook the brown sugar, corn syrup, and milk to softball stage. So far, so good.

I blended shortening with powdered sugar and a little milk. Finally, I poured the hot syrup over the shortening mixture and began beating. Instead of producing a creamy, spreadable consistency, my icing hardened like cement. In tears, I scraped the ruined confection into the trash. I was a failure. The surprise for Daddy was ruined.

Searching my pantry, I found a can of vanilla icing, which included a package of rainbow-colored sprinkles, and decided it would have to do.

God can redeem our failures. I tried to create a special memory for Daddy that day, and guess what? Daddy loved it. When his best friend called to wish him a happy birthday, I overheard him say, "Dave, I have the best birthday cake ever. The icing has sprinkles on top!"

Father, when I fail, You lift me up. As You shower me with grace, let me also show grace in all my interactions as a caregiver.

VIE HERLOCKER

The Privilege of Sharing Burdens

Carry each other's burdens, and in this way
you will fulfill the law of Christ.
—GALATIANS 6:2 (NIV)

A couple of years after my dad was diagnosed with Alzheimer's, he started fretting over financial matters. I lived 6 hours away, so I would try to reassure him by phone. However, on one of my visits, this proud, capable man sat me down and asked if I could help him pay a few bills.

I could tell the request was difficult to make, but he knew it was time. Organized as always, he had set up a card table. The bills were stacked in alternating directions along with the envelopes for mailing. Beside them, he'd put stamps, return address labels, and a pen. He pulled his two checkbooks out of his shirt pocket and handed them to me with instructions to write the checks. Then he pulled out his own pen and said he would sign them.

This was a huge moment for me, too, because it lessened my own worries. Once we had whittled down the stack, he seemed relieved. He kicked back in his recliner and took a nice long nap.

What a blessing to be allowed to do something for my parents, especially for my dad, who'd always taken care of me.

Lord, thank You for how You bless us when we share each other's burdens.
MISSY TIPPENS

Relinquishing Our Candles

**Finally, all of you, be like-minded, be sympathetic,
love one another, be compassionate and humble.**
—1 PETER 3:8 (NIV)

I'm never attending Christmas Eve candlelight service with Grandma again," our 19-year-old son, Cory, proclaimed. "She nearly set me on fire!"

My 92-year-old mother's advancing macular degeneration made seeing in a darkened room especially difficult. But with her fiercely independent, can-do personality, she refused to admit she was no longer capable of doing certain things.

The following Christmas, my mother was thankfully still with us. Several days before the candlelight service, I broke the news to her. "Mom, this year you won't be getting a real candle."

"Why not?" she demanded.

"Because you nearly torched your grandson last year." She denied having done such a thing, but I stood firm. "I'm sorry, Mom. This year you're getting a battery-operated candle."

She finally agreed if she wouldn't be the only one with a plastic candle. "OK," I said. "I'll hold a plastic one too."

As we all sang "Silent Night" at the Christmas Eve service, our counterfeit tapers flickered in the dark sanctuary along with everyone else's. Mom was grateful to participate in the ceremony but seemed a bit sad. To the rest of us, it was just a candle, but to her it was another simple pleasure that aging forced her to relinquish.

That night I added a new prayer to my repertoire:

*Lord, make me more sympathetic to the pain that aging
brings to others, and when my time comes, please help
me relinquish each candle with grace.*

ANDREA ARTHUR OWAN

A Keepsake of Memory

If there is anything worthy of praise, think about these things.
—PHILIPPIANS 4:8 (RSV)

Your mother's cows got out of their fence again!" said the caller. *Can the day get any more complicated?* I complained to myself. Getting the cows back in was my husband's job, but he was away helping a neighbor. I was already late on two work deadlines, and I had yet to fix the daily meal for my mother. In her early eighties, my mother had recently suffered a series of ministrokes that made cooking for herself difficult. We watched her comings and goings closely and brought food to her home daily.

I felt angry and out of control. There were too many things to do, and there was too little time. I drove to my mother's farm, and she walked out into the pasture with me. At least the cows were easier to get back in the fence than I thought.

In the pasture she knew so well, we found a wild plum tree. "I never knew this tree was here," she said, leaning upon her cane.

Suddenly my frustrations fell away. All I saw was my mother reaching for a plum against the backdrop of an azure sky with cranes flying overhead.

Even this difficult day had given me a precious and perfect moment to remember, a keepsake to treasure for the future.

Lord, help me to slow down and look for the beauty in my day.
RAYLENE NICKEL

Long-Haul Caregiving

"Come to me, all you who are weary and burdened,
and I will give you rest."
—MATTHEW 11:28 (NIV)

I looked over the calendar for the month. Several doctor appointments were upcoming for my husband's frail 90-year-old mother. I poked my head into our home office.

"Don't forget your mom's appointment with her internist on Thursday. And are you taking her to her cardiology appointment too?" Mike grumbled an affirmative.

For 23 years, we'd been caring for aging parents. That was a huge chunk of time and a lot of responsibility. My mother and Mike's dad were gone now. Mike was 70, and I was 69. Before long the calendar would likely fill with our own medical woes. Was there no end to this?

Sleep was elusive that night. Resentment grew. I took a sip of water in the dark, and suddenly a still small voice reminded me that it's an honor—not a burden—to care for aging parents. Not everyone gets that privilege. My dad had died at 55. He didn't live long enough to need help in later life, and he wasn't around to care for his own widowed mother.

Caring for aging parents is tiring. Occasional breaks are needed. But in its own divine way, it is a privilege that not everyone gets to share.

Father, when we are feeling the burden of caregiving for our parents,
remind us that it is an honor You have bestowed on us.
SHARON DRACH MANGAS

Picture This

"You have sorrow now, but I will see you again, and your hearts will rejoice, and no one will take your joy from you."
—JOHN 16:22 (ESV)

My sadness deepened with each falling tear. Dealing with Mom's Alzheimer's was difficult for both of us. I was unprepared for the feelings of isolation and exhaustion. I cried quietly, wishing things were different.

I looked around her living room. Pictures covered the tables. As I studied each photo, I was met with glimpses of Mom's past. Some of her favorite moments were captured here as reminders of happier times. There she was looking beautiful on her wedding day, there smiling wide with the three of us children huddled within the folds of her skirt. In another photograph, she knelt, planting iris bulbs in her garden. I realized how much she had given of herself throughout her life.

I started to cry again, but this time, the tears were not born from sadness. Instead, I experienced the joy she felt in each picture, and the memory of her strength filled me with a sense of calm. I knew the days ahead were not going to get any easier, but I now felt certain I could meet each challenge with a renewed spirit.

Lord, help me find strength in the memories
of my loved ones.
JEANNIE HUGHES

Melvin

God loves a cheerful giver.
—2 CORINTHIANS 9:7 (ESV)

My mother-in-law, Clara, has given me wonderful gifts throughout the years, but my favorite is last year's Christmas gift, a coffee mug with the name *Melvin* printed on it.

Clara typically eats at Cracker Barrel on Wednesdays and does her gift shopping there. She bought my husband a mug that has a Marines logo on it, which makes perfect sense because he is a retired vet; however, I don't drink coffee, and my name is not Melvin. I certainly don't know many Melvins, so it's possible that name has been discontinued and was in the closeout bin. Maybe she regifted it, but that would mean somebody else chose to give her a Melvin mug, which seems very unlikely.

Regardless of how I ended up with the Melvin mug, I know that even with the confusion of her Alzheimer's, she still chose this particular gift for me. I never questioned her about it because I didn't want to bring attention to her memory loss or diminish her joy of giving. Every time I take a sip from Melvin, I smile.

Every Christmas that I am able to spend with Clara is a gift. I will always cherish my Melvin mug, knowing that, like every other gift I have received from her, it was given with love.

Lord, thank You for all the gifts in my life,
even when they're a bit of a puzzle.
KRISTY DEWBERRY

Angry Words

A gentle answer turns away wrath,
but a harsh word stirs up anger.
—PROVERBS 15:1 (NIV)

My mother, a retired nurse, lay in a hospital bed not long after knee-replacement surgery. Her pain level was high, but this reluctant patient stubbornly refused to be honest with her nurses.

She was certainly in a daze from her medications, but she was allowed to take additional pain medicine so she could rest and begin to heal. I grew more frustrated each time she refused the help she needed. Every time I told nurses she was in pain, Mom said, "No, I'm fine!" Finally, after several tiring hours of this, I snapped, challenging her. "Mom! The nurses can't help if you aren't honest with them!"

She fired back at me, "You don't need to be here! I don't want you here!"

It was then I realized Mom had no awareness of what was going on around her. And though her words were drug-induced, they still stung. I felt like a complete failure as her caregiver.

A week later, Mom recovered without any memory of the harsh words we'd exchanged. She was even glad I was there. But I remembered our conversation and hoped, with God's help, to speak gently and lovingly to my mother in the future.

*Lord, when I'm worried, remind me to step back and lean
on Your love rather than releasing angry words.*
LORI DURHAM

Missing Pieces

"How can you think of saying to your friend, 'Let me help
you get rid of that speck in your eye, when you can't
see past the log in your own eye?'"
—MATTHEW 7:4 (NLT)

When Mom started losing everything from letters to gift cards, I remained patient. I figured when I'm 92, I might do worse, especially if I have dementia like Mom does. At least her apartment was small, and I could usually find the missing items under the bed or couch cushions.

But all my kind, gracious thoughts vanished when her expensive hearing aids disappeared. We looked for them for weeks with no success.

"How can anyone not keep track of something so important?" I grumbled to my husband. Without the funds to buy new hearing aids, we had to raise our voices three notches to talk with Mom. Every conversation exhausted us.

I needed a break. An upcoming weekend retreat would be the perfect escape. At breakfast on Saturday, one of the ladies drew my name for prayer and wrote me a letter brimming with encouragement and hope. But when I returned home and unpacked, the letter was missing. I searched my suitcase, purse, and book bag. "How can anyone not keep track . . . ?" I began.

That's when I remembered Mom's face, confused and sad. It was time to develop my patience muscles a little more.

*Father, help us remember to grant others grace and patience
just as You have extended it to us.*
JEANETTE LEVELLIE

Together in Spirit

The heavens are telling the glory of God . . .
their voice goes out through all the earth.
—PSALM 19:1, 4 (RSV)

I pushed my mother's wheelchair outside the care center to a place we could sit in the sun. She asked, "Am I ever going to go home again?"

I didn't know how to answer. I had been devastated when a stroke paralyzed her on the right side. Before that, my husband, John, and I had cared for her in her home. My mother was 89, and I had wanted so much for her to spend her last days in her own house. But home care was no longer possible.

I could hardly bear to see her now separated from her family, her treasured backyard birds, and the hills on the horizon at her farm. I visited her often in the care center, but my visits fell far short of easing the sense of loss she must have felt.

One day she asked, "Did you see the moon last night? I was thinking that if you saw the moon at the same time as I did, it would be a way for us to communicate."

At home that night I searched for the moon in the star-studded sky. I realized that even though distance separated us, my mother and I could still be together in spirit by remembering and focusing on those things we both loved.

Lord, please show me how to stay close in spirit
to loved ones separated from me.
RAYLENE NICKEL

Lifting Us Up

Every good and perfect gift is from above, coming down from the Father of the heavenly lights, who does not change like shifting shadows.

—JAMES 1:17 (NIV)

I'm useless!" Mom cried in frustration.

The ones we care for often feel useless as age or disease steals their strength and stamina. It can be difficult to keep their spirits up, especially if they are homebound.

"What if you do something nice for somebody else?" I asked.

"What could I possibly do?" she said a little more harshly than I knew she meant.

"You could call someone. You could invite a friend over and have dinner brought in. You want to send surprise flowers to someone? What about your cards? Are you still sending them?"

Mom loved sending cheery notes to people who needed a lift. She made sure I sent a thank-you card for every gift I got. Now I make the cards I send. As Mom became homebound, I created doubles of my cards, adding the duplicates to Mom's stash.

Parkinson's had affected her hands to the point that her handwriting had diminished to an unreadable scrawl. So I printed various messages for the insides of the cards, applying double-stick tape to the back of each. Mom could pick the appropriate one, peel off the backing, and put the message inside.

Mom wiped the tears from her face. "Let's send flowers! Then you can write a few notes for me," she said. I saw a smile I had not seen in a long time.

Lord, help me today to have words that encourage others
even when things seem overwhelming.

PAMELA HASKIN

Comfort for Caregivers

Brotherly Love

A friend loves at all times, and a brother is born
for a time of adversity.
—PROVERBS 17:17 (NIV)

When my mom had major dental surgery, I thought I could manage her care without the help of my siblings. My sister lived an hour away, one brother lived 30 minutes away, and another brother lived 20 minutes away.

"Don't you want me to take the day off and help you?" William asked.

Timothy said, "I can rearrange my schedule and help you get her home, if you need me."

"I got this," I told both of them.

Arriving at my mom's after the surgery, I saw Timothy's truck in the driveway. But what was he doing here when I'd told him I didn't need his help? He met me at the garage to help her in. She took a couple of steps, but then slowly wilted. Her blood pressure must've dropped, and she almost fainted. It took both of us to get her safely to the recliner.

"Boy, am I glad you were here," I told Timothy after we got Mama settled. "That's the last time I'll try to go it alone."

"We're better together, sis," he said.

"I think you're right."

God, I thank You for the blessing of family and for reminding me
I do not shoulder the burden of caregiving alone.
JULIE LAVENDER

The Elephant in the Room

This is my comfort in my affliction,
for your word has given me life.
—PSALM 119:50 (JPS)

When are we eating lunch?" Mom asked. "I'm starving."
"Really?" I replied. "We just ate. Don't you remember?"
"We didn't have lunch yet," Mom countered. "I'd know if we had already eaten." She was getting testy. She believed in all earnestness that she was right. How could I explain to her Alzheimer's brain that we'd already eaten and also avoid an unnecessary argument? I decided to try logic.

"Look, Mom, those are our lunch dishes in the sink," I said. "We both had a sandwich and salad."

Mom looked at the dishes, then burst into tears. "I don't remember," she cried. "There's something wrong with my brain."

This journey was extremely difficult for both of us. Mom refused to acknowledge her forgetfulness as Alzheimer's, but at the same time she was clearly troubled by her diminished capabilities. She fell into my arms and wept against my shoulder.

I comforted her as best I could and brought her back to the safety of the present. I decided that I had to stop asking her direct questions. It was obvious she didn't remember eating lunch. So instead of, "Don't you remember?" I could say, "I remember you had pastrami on rye and your pickle fell to the floor." There was no ambiguity in that sentence.

As we sat together in the living room, I vowed to strive for clarity in our conversations.

Dear God, grant me patience and wisdom to deal
with my loved one's questions and confusion.
MIRIAM GREEN

Taking Heed

"I have no peace, no quietness; I have no rest, but only turmoil."
—JOB 3:26 (NIV)

I think you are depressed." My doctor's words shocked me, and I protested. I chose to be Daddy's caregiver, and I found joy in all that I did for him. I also loved my job as a school administrator, and with my accumulated leave, I worked flex time to care for Daddy as needed.

My doctor persisted. "How are you really doing?" Her question triggered tears and honesty. Yes, even though I was seeing a counselor, I was floundering. I admitted I could not concentrate at work. Simple tasks overwhelmed me. I slept fewer than 3 hours a night, my mind knotted with worry about Daddy. My cheerful persona shrouded the turmoil within.

I reluctantly agreed to begin a mild antidepressant. Then I hesitated to fill the prescription. I shouldn't be so weak. Why didn't Jesus simply make me better? I prayed for wisdom about the medication, and God's peace came. After a few weeks on the medication, I began sleeping all night. Now that I felt rested, I handled all my responsibilities better and with renewed joy.

Father, help me to remember that while Your healing
may come miraculously, it may also come through
physicians, counselors, and friends.

VIE HERLOCKER

Finding the Right Role

Each of you should use whatever gift you have
received to serve others.

—1 PETER 4:10 (NIV)

When my mother's breast cancer spread to her brain, she was discharged home with hospice care. As a registered nurse for 25 years, I immediately jumped into the role of consummate caregiver. I ordered supplies, organized her medications, and drew up an exhaustive schedule for all her needs.

By the time Debbie, the hospice case manager, arrived, I had collapsed into a chair in tears. "I can't do it all," I said. "I've taken care of patients for all these years, and I want my mother to receive the best too. But I'm just spent."

Debbie took my hand and looked into my eyes with the utmost compassion. "You don't have to, Roberta," she said softly. "That's why you have a hospice team. Each member has their own special gifts. We'll coordinate everything to make sure your mother has whatever she needs. We'll be sending a nursing assistant out to give her a bath. Then when it gets closer to the end, one of our nurses will be right here with you."

Debbie eased over to Mother's bedside and took her hand.

I will never forget her wise words to me. "Why don't you just let all of us love on your mama and you focus on being her daughter now?"

Help me, Lord, to figure out my best role in caregiving.

ROBERTA MESSNER

Always with Us

The LORD is my shepherd; I shall not want.
—PSALM 23:1 (ESV)

My mom and sister had left an hour before for the hospital to see my dad. I'd fed my cats and then followed behind them. I was on the highway when my phone dinged. "How close are you all? His oxygen levels are dropping." It was the group chat for my family. We'd spent the past few days keeping vigil, two at a time, as per COVID regulations.

The text messages kept coming, my sister giving updates. "It's 85. It's 69. It's 65." I had at least another half an hour to go. Tears streaming down my face, I turned the phone off and turned on a song.

"Shepherd me, O God, beyond my wants, beyond my fears, from death into life." The psalm played from my speakers, and I sang along, praying as I drove.

"It's OK, Dad," I said. "You don't have to wait for me. It's OK to go."

The song continued on repeat for 30 minutes. The refrain focused me; the words offered comfort. I arrived, parked. Went in and told security they were expecting me.

As soon as I entered his room, my sister said, "He's gone." Her eyes were red. "We couldn't tell you while you were driving. It was 9:36."

"It's OK. I understand."

Later, I looked at my phone and the timing of the messages. Her last one had come in at 9:32. I'd been talking to my dad when he'd gone, and I knew God had been with him.

Lord, when I can't be there with my loved one, may
I find comfort in knowing that You are there.
MONICA HERALD

A Tough Decision

Blessed are those who mourn, for they will be comforted.
—MATTHEW 5:4 (NIV)

I slipped into the funeral home. Mom was in a nursing home now, under hospice care. It was time to get familiarized with her prepaid funeral arrangements. I dreaded it.

The funeral director greeted me with a kind smile. As we reviewed the paperwork, I started bawling. "Forgive me. I just put Mom in a nursing home, and I'm having a tough time of it. I keep second-guessing myself. It's one of the hardest decisions I've ever made."

He handed me some tissues. "Mrs. Mangas, I've got something you might like to read." He reached into a desk drawer and handed me a book titled *When Love Gets Tough: The Nursing Home Decision* by Doug Manning. We finished our business, I thanked him, and I headed home.

The book was a life-changing read. Doug Manning, a minister, wrote it based on personal experience. He discussed why the decision often has to be made and how patients and their families learn to adjust. The title of the first chapter said it all: "Love Is Doing What People Need—Not What They Want."

I still wished Mom didn't have to be in a nursing home, but after reading Manning's book, I was confident she was where she needed to be. It was the safest place for her. Her physical needs had exceeded my capabilities. I understood now. My decision was born of love, not indifference.

Lord, thank You for help from unexpected places, from those who see our needs and offer comfort in times of sorrow.
SHARON DRACH MANGAS

A Caregiver's Manifesto

Bless those who persecute you; bless and do not curse.
—ROMANS 12:14 (NIV)

My husband, Chris, and I were at the end of our caregiving rope. My mother's naturally combative personality was worsening as her memory faltered. Nearly every interaction exhausted us physically, emotionally, and spiritually.

It didn't help that Mom and I had never enjoyed a warm relationship. I rarely measured up to her expectations. Even at 97, she repeatedly pointed out things she didn't like about me, like how I wasn't around enough or attentive enough. Nearly everything I tried to help her with backfired on me. She also knew how to open old wounds.

I felt racked with guilt. Was I the only daughter on the planet that had such an oil-and-water relationship with her mother and struggled with providing her care?

Then I read an article about the best ways to support difficult family members while saving your own peace of mind. Several tips helped me write a personal caregiver's manifesto.

I would major in kindness and patience and aim to please God in my caregiving, even when Mom threw verbal daggers my way. I would strive to think more like a detached, compassionate caregiver than a dejected, conscience-stricken daughter. And I would stop striving for the unlikely fairy-tale ending of receiving the affirmation and appreciation I so wanted from her.

Lord, help me remember not to take things so personally when I have problems or doubts as a caregiver.
ANDREA ARTHUR OWAN

All Things Work Together for Good

*We know that in all things God works for the good of those
who love him, who have been called according to his purpose.*
—ROMANS 8:28 (NIV)

Mom was in the hospital, her tired heart failing. Her shoulders and arms were so tiny and frail in her thin cotton gown. My husband, our two children, my sister, and I surrounded her bed. It wouldn't be long now. Her breaths grew shallow and further apart. Tears ran down our cheeks. "We're with you, Mom. We love you."

I remembered how, 12 years earlier, I had feared Mom moving in with us. We were different in so many ways. But now, in the space between Mom's final breaths, something incredible happened. Like a gray mist, the distance I'd always felt between the two of us evaporated. I remembered God's whisper earlier in my caregiving journey: *I'm giving you this time with her.*

Despite our differences, by the time Mom passed away at 90, I had grown to respect, appreciate, and love her to a degree I would never have dreamed possible. And here's the thing: Had I not been given the opportunity to observe her closely, day in and day out, as she confronted the challenges and losses associated with aging—including blindness and heart failure—I never would have fully appreciated her strength, optimism, and courage.

I'm giving you this time with her. In the end, our time together was a beautiful and totally unexpected gift.

*Thank You, God, for Your perfect timing and perfect ways.
You can take the most difficult circumstances and
turn them into something beautiful and good.*
KITTY SLATTERY

Warning Sighs

All my longings lie open before you, Lord;
my sighing is not hidden from you.
—PSALM 38:9 (NIV)

When she first came to live with us, my 91-year-old mother sighed with every move she made—up and down stairs, in and out of chairs. Was it her back pain? Was she grieving her husband's death or missing family and friends she'd left behind? Perhaps she felt exasperated with the bleak midwinter gray skies. It seemed likely a combination of these, but when asked, Mom couldn't explain it.

The sighs seemed infectious. During one of his visits, my grandson said to me, "Did you know that you just sighed five times in the last minute?" "I don't think so," I said. "Yes, you did," he said. "I was counting." His comment gave me pause.

Mom and I were both in transition—trying to put together the pieces of this new chapter. Perhaps her sighs were a kind of prayer. We built some routines together, like making meals, doing yard work, and folding laundry. At bedtime, we read a psalm and prayed. Mom eventually stopped sighing and started humming. Even singing. Her growing contentment and happiness put a song in my heart, and I stopped sighing too. We'd both landed on the side of joy.

Lord, thank You for listening to our sighing hearts and guiding us through life's transitions.

JUDY PALPANT

Keeping Watch

Religion that God our Father accepts as pure and faultless
is this: to look after orphans and widows in their distress and
to keep oneself from being polluted by the world.
—JAMES 1:27 (NIV)

My widowed mother, who's 77, kept the phone conversation lighthearted, but I sensed something wasn't right. We lived an hour's drive from each other.

Mom had lost her footing the previous night and fallen to the floor. Luckily, she wasn't injured, but she said it took her an hour to get back on her feet. After numerous attempts, she finally pulled herself up on an armchair.

"Mom, it sounds like your arthritis is worsening. If you'll set up an appointment with your doctor, I'll go with you."

A few days later, in Mom's apartment, I realized the problem was more than bad knees. Housekeeping was never Mom's strong suit, but this was different. The floors throughout her apartment were scattered with tissues and other litter she'd dropped and didn't (couldn't?) pick up. Her ironing board was heaped with laundry, her dining table covered with unopened mail.

At the doctor's office, I slipped a note to the nurse, addressing my concerns. The doctor handled it diplomatically. "Ruth, I haven't seen you in a while. Let's do a physical today. Depending on test results, I might send you to a cardiologist for an evaluation."

Mom eyed me nervously. I patted her hand. "Mom, don't worry. Whatever you need, I'll take care of it. I'm here for you."

Dear God, keep watch over the vulnerable, and give their caregivers the strength and patience to care for them.

SHARON DRACH MANGAS

Bright Moments

A cheerful heart is good medicine.
—PROVERBS 17:22 (NIV)

My mother-in-law sat at the kitchen table while I fixed dinner. Suffering with Alzheimer's, she'd moved in with our family when we realized it wasn't safe for her to live alone.

"I miss Margaret," she said.

Margaret had been her best friend for decades. She loved that they shared the same name, although my mother-in-law had gone by her nickname, Stevie, for as long as I had known her.

She chuckled. "We used to get into all sorts of mischief." I peeled potatoes while Stevie told of their shenanigans on a double date. I laughed as if I were hearing the story for the first time. The truth was I'd heard the same tale several times over the recent days.

After she finished, Stevie sighed. "I miss Margaret."

"I know you do," I said. Then I heard the same story again. Even as Stevie forgot the names of her grandchildren, whom she saw daily for almost 3 years, even as she sometimes stumbled over my name, she never forgot about her friend. She was always eager to share these memories with anyone who would listen.

Some days when she seemed a little down, I would prompt her, "Tell me about your best friend, Margaret."

She would smile. "We used to get into all sorts of mischief. Did I ever tell you about our double date?"

Father, help me guide my loved ones to focus on the bright moments.
EDWINA PERKINS

Wise Counsel

The way of fools seems right to them,
but the wise listen to advice.
—PROVERBS 12:15 (NIV)

I got everything ready for Mom's friend Kerry to help with her caregiving for the day, but no matter how much I organized, I still felt nervous. Mom's schedule hung on the refrigerator, detailing each moment of the day: what time she got up, what she ate, when she should take her medicine.

I placed a notebook and pen on the counter where important notes must be written—questions, concerns, new information from the hospice nurse's visit. I was exhausted—everyone kept telling me I needed a break, but it was going to be hard to let someone else take care of her, even for one day. I was the one who knew how everything should go with her.

A knock at the door signaled that my replacement had arrived early. I showed Kerry the schedule and talked through the routine. She listened carefully, asked insightful questions, and jotted information on her own little notepad. Maybe Mom was right. Her friend seemed like she'd be great doing the job I'd thought only I could do.

Kerry settled on the sofa near Mom. I announced I was leaving, but Mom was chattering so much, I'm not sure she even noticed. Maybe I wasn't the only one who needed a break.

The worry I'd expected to carry at leaving Mom to someone else's care melted away. I was ready to start my day.

Father, thank You for sending wisdom and help
my way, especially when I think I know better.
KAREN SARGENT

Feeling Good

Seek the LORD and his strength; seek his presence continually!
—1 CHRONICLES 16:11 (ESV)

Mom ran a comb through her thin, sparse hair and frowned in disgust.

"You know, Mom, we could ask for help with your hair," I said gently.

"There's nothing we can do about it. It's like twigs on a winter tree."

"How about we pray? God, grant me the serenity to accept the things I cannot change," I began.

She interrupted me. "I don't want to accept it."

"I know you're a fighter, so how about the second part—the courage to change the things we can."

"Can't change a barren mountaintop," Mom said, shaking her head.

"The last line is the most important, don't you think, Mom? And the wisdom to know the difference."

"I suppose," she said. "What I know is I can't get more hair."

"Yes, you can! And I'm going to take you there right now." Fifteen minutes later, we were at a shop in the mall with a sales clerk helping Mom try on wigs.

"Let's try this one," the clerk said. "I think the shape and color will be perfect on you." An hour later we walked to the car with three wigs in different shades and styles. "I'm so excited, sweetie," Mom said. "Thank you!"

Thank You, God, for creative solutions to the things we can change in life.

B.J. TAYLOR

Keeping Things in Perspective

"I, even I, am he who comforts you."
—ISAIAH 51:12 (NIV)

I walked out of my mother-in-law's house, climbed into my car, and slammed the door shut. I was angry.

I'd stopped to help with some chores she needed done, only to be told that I didn't fold her towels right, I used the wrong cleaner for her mirrors, and I threw away perfectly good produce.

I sat in the quiet of the car and wondered why I even tried. I was already late for my daughter's softball game. And I had to go home and finish my own work. I had completed the necessary chores, but all my mother-in-law could do was point out what I did wrong.

Then I remembered she had said she hadn't slept well last night. That explained her stiff movements, irritated mood, and complaining spirit.

I swallowed my hurt feelings, hopped out of the car, and ran back inside. I found her sitting in her recliner. I picked up a quilt, laid it on her lap, and knelt by her chair.

"Take a rest and don't fret about dinner. I'm bringing you mushroom chicken. Your favorite."

My mother-in-law smiled at me. "Thank you, honey."

Dear God, help me to see the person beneath the pain and frustrations and not take things so personally.
KATHY BOYD THOMPSON

The Right Way

I will not leave you.
—DEUTERONOMY 15:16 (JPS)

As we were walking home along the busy street, Mom bolted from me and stepped right into the oncoming traffic.

"Mom!" I yelled. I followed her as she weaved her way across two lanes of traffic, remarkably without getting hurt. When I finally caught up with her, she was walking determinedly in the wrong direction. I grabbed her hand. "Are you OK?"

"I need to go home," she said. Ever since her Alzheimer's diagnosis, my mother could go abruptly from happy to angry in seconds, and it was often hard to dispel those dark moods.

Now she was walking at a super-fast pace as I tried not to lag behind. I began to walk slower, hoping she'd feel the drag of my hand pulling her back. It worked because she slowed down. Then, all of a sudden, she stopped in the middle of the sidewalk.

"I don't know where I am," she cried, panicking.

"I know where we are," I said, stepping up to comfort her. "Look, it's our favorite coffee shop. Let's stop in and rest before we head home."

We sat down in a familiar booth and ordered coffee and ice cream. Never mind that we'd be late getting home or that we'd ruin our appetites for dinner. This was what we both needed after that harrowing episode.

As a sense of calm and joy returned to Mom, I knew we could safely finish our journey home. I had guided her the right way, after all.

Dear God, grant me calm and restraint as I walk my loved one through difficult situations.
MIRIAM GREEN

When Help Isn't Help

Let each of you look not to your own interests
but to the interests of others.
—PHILIPPIANS 2:4 (NRSVUE)

Mom's nursing home provided some kind of activity every afternoon for its residents. Mom's favorite was bingo, and I liked to tag along just to have more time with her. The winners got to pick a favorite bite-size candy bar.

The activity director would call out a number and wait however long it took for the residents to move a colored chip onto their cards. Mom's hands were so impaired that she couldn't open them anymore. She slowly pushed her chips onto her card with the side of her hand.

I struggled watching her difficulty in performing this simple task. Everything in me wanted to help her, but I didn't, no matter how frustrating and heartbreaking it was. Her doctor explained to me that the game was actually a kind of physical therapy. First, it got the residents out of their rooms and interacting with one another. Then it made them have to reach with their arms and shoulders and manipulate their hands and fingers. "She can do it," the therapist assured me. Sometimes the best help is not to help at all.

Lord, thank You for the reminders to let my loved one do
the best that they can, when they are able.
PAMELA HASKIN

Unexpected Consolation

The Lord God will wipe tears away from all faces.
—ISAIAH 25:8 (NASB)

From the ledge next to the hospital room's huge window, I could see Baltimore's skyline. The plan was to stay all day with my dad. I'd brought my laptop, some almonds and chocolate, a book to read. I was too scattered and anxious to do much of anything, though. The book peeked out of my bag, its red-haired protagonist and her hawk looking at me: *Hawkmistress!* by Marion Zimmer Bradley.

My dad lay on the hospital bed, eyes closed, breathing steady. He was unresponsive and hadn't been awake for 2 days. His hair was longer than I'd ever seen it and needed a good trim. When I was growing up, he'd introduced me to Marion Zimmer Bradley and the world of Darkover. Reading was a love we shared, something that he and my mom had both fostered in me.

I had an idea. I hopped off the ledge and dragged a chair next to my dad's bed. I pulled out *Hawkmistress!* and opened to the spot I'd last read. I reached under the blanket for Dad's hand. It was clammy, but I held it and began to read aloud. Slowly at first and then more steadily.

I felt a calm settle over me. My dad had told me stories when I was little, and even though he wasn't alert, I could still be with him, like he'd been with me.

God, when I'm at my wits' end, help me listen to
Your quiet voice and find comfort.
MONICA HERALD

Bridging the Miles

"May the Lord keep watch between you and me
when we are away from each other."
—GENESIS 31:49 (NIV)

I put my pen down and closed the copy of *Walking in Grace*. I wrapped the book in shiny red Christmas paper—a gift for my daddy. I'd also prepared his stocking, filled with gag gifts and gadgets, as I'd done for years.

My husband and I lived in Lucketts, Virginia, and Daddy lived in Athens, Georgia, nearly 600 miles from us. I grieved at being so far away, especially since he was undergoing cancer treatments. We wanted him to come live with us, but he wasn't ready to leave his home. At least we could visit for Christmas.

Daddy always loved his stocking. After he'd reveled in the corny items and retrieved the Hershey's Kisses, I held out one more gift. The book.

God had shown me a way to bridge the miles. Throughout *Walking in Grace*, I'd written notes on special dates—holidays, birthdays, anniversaries—and other notes at random. When I couldn't be with him, the notes would remind him that I loved him and prayed for him daily.

After the holiday, I phoned to say we were safely home. Daddy chuckled and then admitted, "I couldn't wait. As soon as you left, I thumbed through the book and read the notes. Now I can enjoy them twice!"

*Father, thank You for the love notes You share with me throughout
the Bible. Your Word reminds me that You are not far away.*
VIE HERLOCKER

Walking Each Other Home

"Go forth from your . . . land and from your . . . house to the land that I will show you."
—GENESIS 12:1 (JPS)

Mom and I were getting ready for bed. Dad was away at a conference.

"I need to go home," Mom said suddenly.

"This is your home, Mom," I replied, knowing it was her Alzheimer's talking.

"My home is identical to this, but this one is not mine," she said, standing in the middle of her living room.

She was getting agitated. I showed her the family photos and her name on the door. She rebuffed my explanations and angrily demanded I take her home.

It was dark outside. Could I lock the door and walk to another room until she calmed down? Should we leave the apartment? What would happen if I took her outside? I was terrified of her running from me or refusing to return with me, of losing leverage to change the situation.

I decided to chance it. "OK, Mom," I said, "let's put our shoes on." We set out into the night. We left from the front door of the apartment and headed down the street, arm in arm, singing as we went. We turned the corner and continued walking around the block. We approached the building from the back entrance.

"Here's your building," I told her. "Let's go up the elevator to your apartment. Here's your door with your name on it."

Mom walked in, appeased. And I trembled with relief. "Thank you for bringing me home," she said.

*Dear God, may You always lead me and my loved one
safely home through Your love and grace.*
MIRIAM GREEN

Doing the Same for Her

Be shepherds of God's flock that is under
your care, watching over them.
—1 PETER 5:2 (NIV)

I'm ready," my mother called from her room.
"Fold your blanket. I'll be there soon," I shouted back, buying a few more minutes of rest on the couch.

"I can't," she said. My mother had been battling health issues for years, and she flat-out refused to do things for herself anymore. I wondered how much of it was that she couldn't and how much was that she simply wouldn't. Still, I continued to encourage her to try.

But today I was so tired after a long day. "Lord, help me," I pleaded. Then I cried.

I thought about how my mother had devoted her life to her children and loved us so dearly. "OK," I said aloud. "I can do it!" I pulled myself off the couch and went to take Mom to the bathroom and then tuck her into bed. I thought about my childhood and all the times she'd done the same for me.

Once she was settled, I placed her remote within reach and turned off the light. "'Night, Mom. Sleep well." I blew a kiss.

I knew the Lord would take care of me while I was taking care of her.

Lord, help me to remember You'll always be there
to help me with my caregiving.
PAMELA HIRSON

A Multitude of Counselors

Plans fail for lack of counsel, but with many
advisers they succeed.
—PROVERBS 15:22 (NIV)

After my mother fell and broke her collarbone, she couldn't
remember falling or why she was in the hospital. My fears that
she was suffering from dementia were finally confirmed.

At the rehabilitation facility, she became uncooperative. She yelled
and called me horrible names. Nothing I said or did soothed her spirit.
In fact, my presence only seemed to exacerbate her behavior. The staff
had to restrain her.

I went home defeated and heartbroken. My daughter-in-law—a
hospital nurse—offered advice. "Dementia patients often become
more confused and difficult in a new environment, especially around
family members. It's sometimes better if the family stays away for a
while, so the staff can treat the patient without disruption." Mom's
rehab nurses agreed.

But wouldn't staying away make me a horrible daughter? Would
God approve of such behavior? I needed additional counsel. A close
friend—a pastor's wife and experienced social worker—confirmed
the advice.

Staying away for several days gave me time to pray, to put things
in perspective, and to address a number of issues regarding Mom's
future needs. And it helped her calm down and settle into her new
environment and schedule. I was grateful for my counselors who
weren't afraid to offer some tough but beneficial guidance.

*Thank You, Lord, for the wisdom of those with more
experience than I have, for perspective that lights
my way and relieves the pressures and confusion.*
ANDREA ARTHUR OWAN

Words

May these words of my mouth and this meditation of my heart
be pleasing in your sight, Lord, my Rock and my Redeemer.
—PSALM 19:14 (NIV)

Emptying junk emails from my inbox is one of the least favorite parts of my day. As I scrolled and deleted, I hesitated at one advertisement. The subject line read "Edwina, we're proud of you!" As strange as it may sound, I felt encouraged by those words as if I'd reached an accomplishment and was being acknowledged, even though I knew it was a ploy to get me to open the email. Words of encouragement, no matter where they come from, can feel like an oasis in the desert.

For 3 years, my mother-in-law, Stevie, lived with us while she battled the late stages of Alzheimer's. Once when I brought home ice cream, she clapped her hands like a child and said, "Butter pecan? Thank you so much! You must really love me to buy my favorite ice cream." I stopped putting away the groceries and looked at her sitting in her chair. We'd had a hard week together, and her words soothed my wounded heart.

For some reason, the email's subject line reminded me of times Stevie expressed appreciation. Those times decreased as the disease took over her mind, but the memories remain. That email is still in my inbox—not because I need the accolades from a company that doesn't know me but as a reminder. If I need to be encouraged, so do others.

Father, let the words of my mouth (or even an email)
be used to encourage others.
EDWINA PERKINS

New Realities

Fear not, for I am with you; be not dismayed, for I am
your God; I will strengthen you, I will help you.
—ISAIAH 41:10 (ESV)

Because we lived so far apart, Mom and I only saw each other every few months. She had moved into a nursing home since my last visit. I never imagined my first visit there would be so difficult for me. When I found Mom having lunch in the cafeteria with a few other residents, I gave her a quick hug. Then, suddenly, I was fighting back tears that caught me completely off guard. I knew her health had declined, but it broke my heart to see her needing this level of care. "I'll let you finish your lunch now," I said to her, squeezing back the tears. "I'll meet you in your room after." I made a dash for the door before she could see me crying.

The Lord knows we will face tough times like this and worse in our caregiving journey and in life. That's why He reminds us so many times in Scripture that He will never leave us. I dried my tears, then looked around Mom's room. Photos and crosses from her home decorated the pale yellow walls. Her favorite clothes hung neatly in a closet. She had a TV and a refrigerator filled with her favorite drinks and snacks.

Mom soon joined me in her room. "Come with me and meet my new friend. She lives in the next wing over." I smiled and followed her. If she could adjust to this new reality, so could I.

*Lord, when I'm feeling overwhelmed by big changes in
my caregiving journey, thank You for helping me adjust.*
PAMELA HASKIN

Don't Borrow Trouble

"Therefore do not worry about tomorrow, for tomorrow will worry about itself. Each day has enough trouble of its own."
—MATTHEW 6:34 (NIV)

I know they're not really there," my mom said, scratching the edge of the hospital bed. "But I see spiders crawling." Mom had been in the hospital for weeks after a simple scope went awry and nicked her bile duct, leaking caustic fluids into her body. The strong painkillers she took created vivid hallucinations, like spiders in the bed, mice on the wall clock, and snakes on the floor.

Normally, Mom is terrified of these kinds of critters, of pretty much anything that slithers or creeps. Yet even in critical condition, she understood the nurse's explanations and recognized the visions as hallucinations. She was not afraid.

Unlike my siblings and me. We had more questions than answers.

"What if the problem recurs when she goes home?"

"What if we don't know how to flush the PICC line?"

"What if the pain never goes away?"

It finally dawned on us that we were borrowing trouble; we were anticipating problems that didn't exist yet and feeding unfounded fears. If my mom could ignore the fear of things she knew weren't really there, then we could stop worrying about the "what ifs."

God, help me not to fear the unknown and help me trust what
I do know—that You are with me every step of the way.

JULIE LAVENDER

Loving Touches

A time to embrace, and a time to refrain from embracing.
—ECCLESIASTES 3:5 (NKJV)

I stared at a poster on the bulletin board of Mom's assisted-living facility. "People need four caring touches a day to stay emotionally healthy." Oh, my goodness. Mom barely received four loving touches a week. She got those when she felt well enough to attend church. Maybe five, if you counted the hug I gave her each Wednesday when I ate lunch with her. I doubted she received many touches from anyone else during the week. Her emotional gas tank must be running on fumes.

I tried to think of how I could add more loving touch to Mom's life. We'd never been a huggy family. What could I do to help fill her heart with happiness and at the same time not make us both uncomfortable? The solution came to me almost by accident.

Because Mom's hearing had declined over the last few years, I often had to get close to her ear when we chatted. One day at lunch, instead of simply moving close, I put my arm around Mom's shoulder, and this gave me the opportunity to touch her several times during each conversation. I sometimes even gently cupped her ear forward so she could hear better.

It wasn't the recommended four caring touches a day, but it was a start. One that filled my emotional gas tank too.

Lord, help me remember this caregiving journey is not about what makes me comfortable. Please help me do whatever gives the most grace to my loved one.
JEANETTE LEVELLIE

If You Only Knew

*"I have loved you with an everlasting love; I have drawn
you with unfailing kindness."*
—JEREMIAH 31:3 (NIV)

Our plane landed. Home at last. Checking my phone, I read a text
from my sister: "Call me when you arrive." I did.

"Come straight to the rehab center before going home," she said.
"Mom is failing fast."

The 30-minute drive took forever. I wondered what we'd face
upon arrival. Entering the room, I hugged my sister. Tears filled her
eyes. "Mom has not been responding today," she said. We got the
update from the nurse. Had we returned just in time to say our final
goodbyes?

Mom suddenly opened her eyes and said, "Well, Judy! You're
home. Where have you been?"

Surprised, I said, "We flew to Texas, Mom."

"That's a big place," she said with a smile. Our eyes locked. Then
she exclaimed, "I wish you knew how much I love you!" My heart
skipped a beat. We wouldn't be saying goodbye today. Mom had
rallied once again.

With great relief, our spirits perked up. I told Mom about our
trip. She wanted to hear details about her granddaughter and great-
grandchildren. Later we headed home with gratitude for another day,
pondering life's mysteries.

Mom's journey to her heavenly home came a few weeks later.
But I will always cherish the beauty of her love expressed for me that
day—a mother's fathomless love for her child.

Lord, open my heart to receive love from You as well as from others.
JUDY PALPANT

Strength for the Journey

"The LORD is my strength and my defense."
—EXODUS 15:2 (NIV)

Hold it, please." I rushed to open the car door for my father when we parked. Operation "Get Dad to the Barber Safely" required ensuring that I had the car keys in my pocket, my purse over my shoulder, and the walker from the trunk, wheeled and locked in front of Dad, all before he decided to get out of the car on his own. My father suffered from Alzheimer's, and normally when I walked with him along the hallway of his assisted-living facility, I would almost trip over my feet because we were progressing so slowly. But when he wanted to get out of the car, it was another story. I had to perform at an Olympic sprinter's speed to prevent him from falling out of the car. He would forget he needed help to get out, just like he would forget to unbuckle his seat belt.

Some days I wondered if I had the strength. I'd cry to God, "Help me." This was one of those days.

After we finished our errands and were driving home, Dad said, "Honey, I appreciate all you do for me. I love you."

His words filled my heart. "Oh, Dad, I love you too. I wish I could make things better." I realized that my role was to serve my dad in whatever capacity he needed. His moment of lucidity was God's answer to providing me with strength.

Thank You, God, for knowing just what we need
in order to have the strength to care for others.
VIRGINIA RUTH

Two Equals One

There are different kinds of working, but in all of them
and in everyone it is the same God at work.
—1 CORINTHIANS 12:6 (NIV)

I don't have to go," Mom protested as my sister, a nurse, escorted her to the bathroom, explaining how quickly a urinary tract infection could set in and how serious it could be.

I added that mental note to the other medical facts I had learned from her as we tag-teamed caring for our mom. My sister knew how to change sterile dressings, adjust medications, and check vital signs. I felt like an inadequate caregiver.

But when it came to providing emotional support, my sister felt inadequate. As an ER nurse, she'd learned to tamp down her feelings so she could provide the best care for her patients. To keep her heart from conflicting with her head, she focused on Mom's medical needs.

I focused on Mom's emotional needs. When she was afraid to sleep alone, I snuggled beside her. When she reminisced about the past or imagined what heaven would be like, I listened. When she craved physical touch, I held her hands or embraced her.

In our exhaustion and the stressful situation, it would have been easy for my sister to think I left the hardest jobs for her. Or I could have criticized her for often escaping to the other room.

Instead, I'm thankful for her knowledge, and in turn I could do the things for our mom that were more difficult for my sister.

Thank You, Lord, for giving us different gifts so we can meet the needs of others.

KAREN SARGENT

Attitude Adjustment

Give thanks in all circumstances; for this is
God's will for you in Christ Jesus.
—1 THESSALONIANS 5:18 (NIV)

After Mom broke her hip, she needed someone to stay with her day and night. I moved in to make sure she had her meals, took her pills, and did the physiotherapy. Every morning before I got her out of bed, I would get her to do the exercises, something we both hated. She didn't want to do them, and all the coaxing exhausted me.

"C'mon, Mom," I'd say. "You need to lift that leg to a 45-degree angle."

One morning she exploded. "Stop bossing me. I'm the mother! And what's this about angles?!"

I turned away from her and walked toward the window. *God*, I silently prayed, *this will never work!* Seven flights down in the park, I could see children playing flag football. I could see the coach waving his arms and pointing and then a child running in that direction. I took a deep breath and turned back to Mom.

"Mom, I'm not bossing you. I'm your coach. This is the bed," I said holding my palm flat. "This is a 45-degree angle." I demonstrated with the other palm on top.

She smiled. "I see. Well, Coach, let's get this done before breakfast!" I smiled back. A simple change in our attitudes had made all the difference.

*Lord, thank You for showing me that with an attitude
of gratitude and patience, I can best help others.*
B'ETTE SCHALK

A Way In

A [child] should honor his father.
—MALACHI 1:6 (JPS)

Now that Mom was in an Alzheimer's care facility, I needed to figure out ways to begin caring for Dad without being too obvious. At 82, he was lucid and capable of caring for himself, but was he lonely? Did he need my assistance? Although he visited Mom every day, Dad's nights were often solitary. He had his books, his favorite shows, and the scientific work he'd kept up with, but general conversations were infrequent.

"I'm going shopping tomorrow," I said on the phone. "Can I buy your groceries too?"

"Yes, please," he said.

This is my way in, I thought, as I made his list. When I was at the store, I bought enough salmon for a family meal. I decided I'd go by his house one afternoon, cook dinner, and invite the family to join us. It would be strange to cook in Mom's kitchen without her but an ideal way to critically view what Dad might need.

Dinner was a success. Two grandchildren joined us, and we had a lively evening with banter and laughter. There were even leftovers for him to have during the week.

"Thank you for this lovely evening," he said, taking my hand. "I've missed my home being joyful."

That's when I knew that the weekly efforts to gather Dad into the family fold would be a springboard to whatever came next. I would be ready.

Dear God, guide me to ascertain and meet my loved one's needs.
MIRIAM GREEN

Making Hard Decisions with Love

I pray that you, being rooted and established in love, may have power, together with all the Lord's holy people, to grasp how wide and long and high and deep is the love of Christ.
—EPHESIANS 3:17–18 (NIV)

The group text between us six siblings was in full swing from Colorado to Maryland, a whirlwind of different opinions about what to do regarding our father. Dad had been hallucinating for several months, and the decisions about hospitals and rehabs were wearing on us all. Today, the conversation was about his imminent return to a rehab facility and which one we should choose. Stakes were high.

We all had different ideas about what "taking care of Dad" looked like. His complicated in-between status didn't help. He was out of rehab days and not yet approved by Medicaid. Insurance limbo.

My brother: "I spoke with several places, and there's one I think will work. But they said he can't apply for a move until his Medicaid goes through."

My sister: "You didn't see him. They'll kill him. I've worked in those places and seen it happen."

Back and forth as quickly as fingers could type, with increasing frequency and disagreement and even rancor.

Until another brother wrote this: "Just want to remind everyone, this is stressful for everybody. Some of us have been working nonstop and still going to the hospital daily. Let's all take a breath." We were all trying to watch out for Dad in the best ways we could, both individually and as a group, and that was far more important than our disagreements.

God, when I am angered by those with whom I'm sharing caregiving decisions, help me root myself in love.
MONICA HERALD

Pictures of Happiness

*This is the reason we do not give up. Our human body is
wearing out. But our spirits are getting stronger every day.*
—2 CORINTHIANS 4:16 (NLV)

Mom was having a good day. Some days she knew I was her
daughter, and other days, she believed I was a hired caregiver.

As we looked through a family photo album that afternoon, she
studied each picture. "Oh, look, there's Kelly," she said, pointing to
a photo.

"Yes, that's right," I encouraged her.

She smiled. "That was a fun time."

It had been 4 months since my brother and his family had been
for a visit. I could still hear the excited voices of his grandchildren as
yet another bag hit its mark in a friendly game of cornhole. These were
the last pictures taken with Mom participating in family life.

Her days of lucidity were becoming farther apart, so I cherished the
moments when she still knew who we were. It was special when she
remembered what it was like to be a part of a family.

I turned the pages in the album. I was so excited she was able to
pick out a picture of my sister, Kay, too.

"Remember how Kay took us all for ice cream that day?" I asked
Mom.

"I do remember that!" she said.

Yes, this was a very good day.

*Lord, thank You for the precious moments of peace
brought by happy memories.*
JEANNIE HUGHES

Finding the Best Ways to Help

Offer hospitality to one another without grumbling.
—1 PETER 4:9 (NIV)

When I received an email from the director at Mom's assisted-living facility, my heart rate doubled. What now? I hope she hasn't left her stove burner on again. But this time it was only a request to help Mom pick up the mounds of clutter in her apartment so the cleaning staff could dust and vacuum.

I'd noticed the unfinished letters, half-read books, and $5 bills piled haphazardly everywhere—on the coffee table, kitchen counter, living room floor. Once an efficient accounting clerk, Mom had lost her ability to organize. I would've jumped right in and decluttered on my frequent visits, except that Mom did not want help. She'd lost so much independence in the last few years. If I offered to tidy up her apartment, she'd take it as a criticism that she couldn't manage on her own. So I got sneaky.

When I knew Mom was playing bingo in the dining room, I let myself into her apartment. I sorted and tossed junk mail, ancient church bulletins, and expired coupons. I dumped spoiled food from her fridge. I put dirty clothes left on the bathroom floor into the hamper.

One day when I showed up for lunch, Mom waved her hand over the room like a game show hostess displaying expensive prizes. Her eyes shone. "Did you notice how nice and neat my house looks today? I cleaned it up for your visit."

My secret was safe.

Lord, I realize this caregiving gig is not about me.
Please give me creative ways to help.
JEANETTE LEVELLIE

My Anchor

Do not cast me away when I am old; do not
forsake me when my strength is gone.
—PSALM 71:9 (NIV)

Sharon, I have an awful sore throat. It might be a tooth." Mom was
getting frailer. These days, new health issues emerged weekly. As
soon as one thing was under control, something else popped up.

It wasn't a tooth. Mother had a bad case of shingles. It was in her
throat, earlobes, nostrils, eyes, and scalp, causing terrible pain. The
doctor prescribed medication and sent us home. He told me she'd
need someone with her the next few weeks. How would I manage
that? My husband and I worked full-time.

Mom worsened and ended up hospitalized. A caseworker took me
aside and told me that she was eligible for nursing home care. It was
the best option right now. My mother needed round-the-clock care. I
dreaded breaking the news to her.

I sat next to her hospital bed, holding her hand. "I don't want you
in a nursing home, Mom, but I don't know what else we can do right
now. It feels like I'm abandoning you."

She squeezed my fingers. "Sharon, you've always been there for
me. Don't feel guilty. I need more help than you can give right now. It
will be OK."

My plan was to reassure my mother, but instead, she was the one
comforting me. My mom was my anchor of faith, in good times and bad.

*God, we thank You for the blessing of parents. Let us lean on Your wisdom
and the wisdom of others, especially in situations beyond our control.*
SHARON DRACH MANGAS

All the Pretty Shoes

Therefore encourage one another and build
each other up, just as in fact you are doing.
—1 THESSALONIANS 5:11 (NIV)

I'll never get to wear pretty shoes again," Mom lamented to me as I helped her out of her big, clunky orthopedic shoes and the brace she had to wear. Parkinson's had twisted and curled her foot awkwardly. Mom had always loved shoes, sometimes buying several colors of ones she really liked.

It's tough to watch someone you love struggling to adjust to new and growing limitations. I reached out to stroke Mom's cheek. "You're so pretty," I told her, trying not to cry. And it was true—her skin was still smooth and soft from years of faithful moisturizing. I held her shaking hands. Though Parkinson's had affected them as much as her feet, they were still lovely, but her long nails were missing their usual bright polish.

"I'll be right back!" I said. From Mom's large collection of colors, I grabbed a bottle of bright red nail polish. I plopped down on the floor in front of her. I unfolded one finger at a time and painted each nail. I also managed to get polish on her cuticles and the sides of her fingers.

"Couldn't have done it better myself," Mom said with a wink and a smile.

The truth was Mom would never be able to wear her pretty shoes again. But she still made sure she had even those clunky orthopedic shoes in both black and white. Oh, and bright red nails!

*Lord, Creator of all that is beautiful, thank You for helping
me see and nurture the beauty in others.*

PAMELA HASKIN

A Simple Answer

If any of you lacks wisdom, you should ask God, who gives
generously to all without finding fault, and it will be given to you.
—JAMES 1:5 (NIV)

I paced the hallway outside my mother's hospital room. There were
so many questions. Decisions to be made. Doctors said one thing.
Family said another. But I was the caregiver, the one responsible.

Weeks passed, and she cycled better and worse. I prayed for
wisdom, but fear had me locked in a vise. How could I hear God's still
small voice over everyone's chatter in my head?

I'd pack my lunch and spend hours at the hospital. We'd watch
television and talk if Mom wanted to, but mostly we just spent time
together.

I spied a doctor I knew from another wing. Like sunshine in
the midst of a storm, his presence there was odd. We'd had many
discussions in the past, so I gave him a brief history of events and
revealed my unrest.

He said, "When you have a strong belief system, answers are
easy." Then he patted my arm and strode away.

There was truth in that simple wisdom. I'd let myself be swayed,
forgotten my rudder—my belief system. God is not the author of
confusion. He's given me a sound mind and a loving heart. And today,
He sent a messenger to remind me. The Lord's peace washed through
me. The mental chatter had stilled. Fear was gone. Clarity prevailed.

Lord, Your Word is a lamp unto my feet. Thanks
for reminding me and sending wisdom.
PAMELA HIRSON

Honoring What Is Special

Be completely humble and gentle; be patient,
bearing with one another in love.
—EPHESIANS 4:2 (NIV)

"Put these in for me," Mom said, holding up a pair of aqua earrings. They were a Christmas gift from my son, Steven. Mom only wore these earrings on special occasions.

We were going to the grocery store. As her Alzheimer's had progressed, the store had become her favorite outing. She could no longer make a grocery list and often wanted products we already had at home, but this weekly routine still gave her a sense of accomplishment.

She slowly pushed our cart down each aisle, examining every item. I wanted to tell her to hurry up. Grocery shopping should not take 2 hours. I had to keep reminding myself that this was her only outing for the week, and it was important to her.

Checking out with our groceries was no faster. She kept trying to engage the clerk in conversation. What should have been a quick trip to the store had taken up my entire morning.

When we finally got home, Mom put her groceries away and then told me, "Now put my earrings back." As I placed them carefully in her jewelry box, I admired their beauty. It was as if I were seeing them for the first time. I realized they weren't merely an accessory for her; they were a special gift to be worn on the days that meant so much to her. Days that would now mean so much to me.

Lord, please grant me the patience and wisdom to discern
what is most special to my loved ones.
JEANNIE HUGHES

No Place for Shame

Let me not be put to shame, LORD, for I call upon You.
—PSALM 31:17 (NASB)

Linda, a woman in my caregivers' support group, stared at me across the conference room table. "Even though my mom treated my sister Penny unkindly, Penny still takes care of her with all the love and respect *Mom deserves*," she said. As she emphasized the last two words, everyone nodded and made approving sounds. Everyone but me. I sat in my place, anger hammering at my heart.

My muscles tensed with that old feeling of shame. The shame I felt when I was six and my mother yelled at me as my cousin looked on. Or embarrassed me in front of my friends when she corrected my manners. *How dare Linda single me out in front of all these people*, I thought. My comment a minute earlier about how I struggled to keep my patience with my hard-to-please mom was a plea for help. Not an invitation for Linda to scold me in front of others.

Just as I was thinking I'd never come back to this group—I'd find a new one—our leader, Carolyn, spoke up. "It sounds like your mom has always been a difficult person, Jeanette." When I nodded hard, she asked the group to share some tips that had worked for them. Several encouraged me with ideas to make my relationship with Mom easier. To help erase the shame.

I decided to keep coming back.

Lord, You see my motives better than anyone does. Please take away any shame I feel and help me focus on what I'm doing right as a caregiver.
JEANETTE LEVELLIE

Moving through Loss

Record my misery; list my tears on your scroll—
are they not in your record?
—PSALM 56:8 (NIV)

I continued on my brisk 3-mile walk and wiped away tears as quickly as they fell. I tried to focus on the music flowing through my headphones, but my memories were louder. My thoughts floated back to my mom, whom I'd lost over 2 decades ago. I thought about the beauty of her olive skin and the contrast to my own deeper brown.

The tears flowed as I remembered several losses I'd experienced over the years. Losses of parents and in-laws and most recently my dog, Beethoven.

I've learned as a caregiver that loss brings about change in my "normal" routine. I've given myself permission to grieve not only the loss of a loved one but also the changes it brings to my life. Sometimes the changes are the hardest part for me to deal with.

After I finished my walk, I took a few minutes to look at my favorite picture of Mom and me. I smiled and whispered, "I love you."

I rested my hand on the back of the chair where Beethoven had spent most of his days while I worked. I brushed my fingertips across the seat cushion where he'd rested. "I miss you, dear friend," I said.

My tears had stopped—for now, anyway. I took a deep breath before getting ready for my day.

Father, help me to move gracefully through the changes
in my life that loss brings.
EDWINA PERKINS

Glimpses of Heaven

He performs wonders that cannot be fathomed,
miracles that cannot be counted.
—JOB 5:9 (NIV)

The hospice nurse broke the news gently. "It's nearing the end now. Don't be surprised if you hear your mother talking to people who are long gone. This happens a lot near death when our loved ones have one foot in this world and one in the next."

My son, Russ, arrived from Chicago a few days later for a last visit with his beloved grandmother. He took a sleeping bag along to the nursing home and told his grandma he was spending the night. "I'm right here if you need me, Grandma."

The next morning, Russ discussed his overnight visit with his dad and me. "It was weird. Grandma talked to Grandpa Herman all through the night." (A chill went through me. My dad had been gone for 50 years.) "But then," Russ continued, "she'd call out for me sometimes . . . 'Russie, are you there?' It was like she was with Grandpa but wanted to check to make sure she was still in this world too. I held her hand when she called out and let her know I was there."

Until Russ shared his experience, I had written off hospice patients speaking with long-gone loved ones as a medical issue caused by diminishing brain function. But now I felt differently. When Mother died 5 days later, I was sure God's hand had been there, preparing her for heaven. I was comforted knowing God had chosen my daddy to call her home.

Lord, thank You for glimpses of heaven that strengthen our faith.
SHARON DRACH MANGAS

Author Index

Acknowledgments

Every attempt has been made to credit the sources of copyrighted material used in this book. If any such acknowledgment has been inadvertently omitted or miscredited, receipt of such information would be appreciated.

Scripture quotations marked (CEB) are taken from the *Common English Bible*. Copyright © 2011 by Common English Bible.

Scripture quotations marked (CEV) are taken from *Holy Bible: Contemporary English Version*. Copyright © 1995 by American Bible Society.

Scripture quotations marked (ESV) are taken from the *Holy Bible, English Standard Version*. Copyright © 2001 by Crossway Bibles, a division of Good News Publishers. Used by permission. All rights reserved.

Scripture quotations marked (JPS) are taken from *Tanakh: A New Translation of the Holy Scriptures according to the Traditional Hebrew Text*. Copyright © 1985 by the Jewish Publication Society. All rights reserved.

Scripture quotations marked (KJV) are taken from the *King James Version of the Bible*.

Scripture quotations marked (NASB and NASB1995) are taken from the *New American Standard Bible*. Copyright © 1960, 1962, 1963, 1968, 1971, 1972, 1973, 1975, 1977, 1995 by The Lockman Foundation, La Habra, California. Used by permission.

Scripture quotations marked (NIV) are taken from *The Holy Bible, New International Version*. Copyright © 1973, 1978, 1984, 2011 by Biblica, Inc. Used by permission of Zondervan. All rights reserved worldwide. zondervan.com

Scripture quotations marked (NKJV) are taken from *The Holy Bible, New King James Version*. Copyright © 1982 by Thomas Nelson.

Scripture quotations marked (NLT) are taken from the *Holy Bible, New Living Translation*. Copyright © 1996, 2004, 2007 by Tyndale House Foundation. Used by permission of Tyndale House Publishers Inc., Carol Stream, Illinois. All rights reserved.

Scripture quotations marked (NLV) are taken from the *New Life Version*. Copyright © 1969, 2003 by Barbour Publishing, Inc.

Scripture quotations marked (NRSVUE) are taken from *New Revised Standard Version, Updated Edition*. Copyright © 2021 National Council of Churches of Christ in the United States of America. Used by permission. All rights reserved worldwide.

Scripture quotations marked (RSV) are taken from the *Revised Standard Version of the Bible*, copyright © 1946, 1952, and 1971 the Division of Christian Education of the National Council of the Churches of Christ in the United States of America. Used by permission. All rights reserved.

Scripture quotations marked (TLB) are taken from *The Living Bible*. Copyright © 1971 by Tyndale House Publishers, Inc., Carol Stream, Illinois. All rights reserved.

A Note from the Editors

We hope you enjoyed *Comfort for Caregivers*, published by Guideposts. For over 75 years, Guideposts, a nonprofit organization, has been driven by a vision of a world filled with hope. We aspire to be the voice of a trusted friend, a friend who makes you feel more hopeful and connected.

By making a purchase from Guideposts, you join our community in touching millions of lives, inspiring them to believe that all things are possible through faith, hope, and prayer. Your continued support allows us to provide uplifting resources to those in need. Whether through our communities, websites, apps, or publications, we inspire our audiences, bring them together, and comfort, uplift, entertain, and guide them. Visit us at guideposts.org to learn more.

We would love to hear from you. Write us at Guideposts, P.O. Box 5815, Harlan, Iowa 51593 or call us at (800) 932-2145. Did you love *Comfort for Caregivers*? Leave a review for this product on guideposts. org/shop. Your feedback helps others in our community find relevant products.

Find inspiration, find faith, find Guideposts.

Shop our best sellers and favorites at
guideposts.org/shop
Or scan the QR code to go directly to our Shop

Printed in the United States
by Baker & Taylor Publisher Services